Calibration Inspections

201
Q&A

SAP Certified Application Associate
PLM-QM

ALSO BY BILLIE G. NORDMEYER

DEFECTS RECORDING
201 Q&A
SAP CERTIFIED APPLICATION ASSOCIATE – PLM-QM

DYNAMIC MODIFICATION
201 Q&A
SAP CERTIFIED APPLICATION ASSOCIATE – PLM-QM

INSPECTION LOT COMPLETION
201 Q&A
SAP CERTIFIED APPLICATION ASSOCIATE – PLM-QM

INSPECTION METHODS & CATALOGS
201 Q&A
SAP CERTIFIED APPLICATION ASSOCIATE – PLM-QM

QUALITY CERTIFICATES
201 Q&A
SAP CERTIFIED APPLICATION ASSOCIATE – PLM-QM

QUALITY COSTS
201 Q&A
SAP CERTIFIED APPLICATION ASSOCIATE – PLM-QM

SAMPLE DETERMINATION
201 Q&A
SAP CERTIFIED APPLICATION ASSOCIATE – PLM-QM

STABILITY STUDIES
201 Q&A
SAP CERTIFIED APPLICATION ASSOCIATE – PLM-QM

TEST EQUIPMENT MANAGEMENT
201 Q&A
SAP CERTIFIED APPLICATION ASSOCIATE – PLM-QM

Calibration Inspections
201
Q&A

SAP Certified Application Associate
PLM-QM

Billie G. Nordmeyer, MBA, MA

First Edition, 2014

Library of Congress Cataloging in Publication Data has been applied for.

ISBN 13: 978-1503137240
ISBN 10: 1503137244

Trademarks

Terms that are referred to in this book, which are known trademarks or service marks, are capitalized. The trademarks are the property of their owners. The inclusion in the book of any term that is a known trademark should not be thought to affect the validity of the trademark. The author of this book is not associated with any product or vendor mentioned in this book.

SAP EC is neither the author nor the publisher of this book, or affiliated with the author or publisher of this book in any way. Nor is SAP EC responsible for the content of the book. The book's content reflects the views of the author and not that of SAP EC. Any omissions or inaccuracies that might be present in this book, which do not correctly depict SAP EC or its products, are purely accidental, without maleficent intent.

Warning and Disclaimer

The author and publisher of this book have taken every precaution to ensure the content of the book is accurate and complete. Neither the author nor the publisher, however, assume any responsibility for inaccurate or inadequate information or for errors, inconsistencies or omissions in this book. Nor do the author or publisher assume any liability or responsibility to any person or entity for any damages or losses that result from the use of information published in this book. Neither the author nor the publisher guarantees that the use of the book will ensure that a candidate will pass any exam.

About the Author

B. G. Nordmeyer, MBA, MA is an SAP consultant, trainer and published author. She has held Senior Consultant and Business Development Manager of SAP Practice positions with a "Big 4" consulting firm, three "Fortune 100" firms and six "Fortune Most Admired Companies." Nordmeyer has consulted with Fortune 100 and Fortune 500 enterprises and supported clients in the aerospace, oil and gas, software, retail, pharmaceutical and manufacturing industries. Nordmeyer holds a BSBA in accounting, an MBA in finance and an MA in international management.

CONTENTS

INTRODUCTION

A technical certification is a valuable achievement in part because employers consider it confirmation that a job candidate is a well-qualified professional. Accordingly, if your goal is a position with a consulting firm, a major firm in industry or a leading not-for-profit organization, SAP certification training will help you get there. SAP training aimed at enhancing your understanding of particular concepts so you might sit for a standardized exam and obtain a professional credential is available both online and at bricks-and mortar institutions. But some training programs fail to accomplish the key objective…namely, prepare a candidate to achieve a passing grade on a certification exam.

In an exam setting, you must identify correct answers to questions that may bear little resemblance to the way major concepts are presented in the day-to-day operation of SAP applications. Consequently, while in your professional life you may play a key role in support of SAP software and solutions, to do well on the exam, you'll need training that provides a global view of interrelated functions and activities. But some training programs fail to provide a certification candidate either the information needed to perform well during a testing process or the means necessary to identify his training needs.

You should also be aware that SAP certification exams assume that, as a certification candidate, you're knowledgeable about definitions and master data, as well as the application of a fairly extensive set of transactions and customizing functions. For example, during the testing process, you may be expected to recognize specific attributes of major transactions and customizing functions, definitions of key system elements, the interrelationship among all of these factors, or other characteristics of the system to which you may not be exposed on a daily basis. Your training program, however, may fail to provide a sufficient number of questions and explanations for you to learn or confirm your knowledge of even the most perfunctory concepts addressed by the certification exam.

What's more, when sitting for the certification exam and the answer to each question is one of several different -- and often complex -- alternatives, you want to be assured ahead of time that you can make the right choice. Reviewing documentation or working through a relatively small number of practice test questions, however, may not provide you with the practical skills needed to apply your knowledge in a multiple-choice testing environment.

Hence this book series for the SAP Certified Application Consultant PLM-QM exam that allows you to enhance and test your knowledge using hundreds of multiple-choice questions well before you take the actual exam. The 201 Q&A SAP Certified Application Consultant PLM-QM book series is composed of individual books, each of which addresses one module, scenario or master data that may be covered in the certification exam. In turn, each study guide, such as Calibration Inspections, provides both a short and detailed answer for each of the 201 questions included in the book. These explanations allow you to grasp the bigger picture, connect new information with prior knowledge and use this knowledge to increase your score on the actual exam.

In the case that you want to review and analyze your knowledge pertaining to only one topic, you can purchase the one book that addresses that topic. If instead, you want to review a number of topics the exam may address, you can purchase some or all of the books in the series. In either case, using the 201 practice exam questions provided in each book, you can analyze your training needs in regards to one function, scenario or master data and then focus your study on the specific areas where you need to enhance your knowledge. In either case, I wish you the best of luck on the exam!

CHAPTER I

QUESTIONS

QUESTIONS

Q-01:   A customer wants to implement the calibration inspection functionality. What do they need to consider? Select all that apply.

A. The implementation of the PP Technical Objects, PP Preventive Maintenance and PP Maintenance Processing components

B. The implementation of the QM Quality Planning and Test Equipment Management components

C. The implementation of the Classification System component

Short Answer: 113
Answer & Explanation: 135

Q-02:   A company runs both the Quality Management and Plant Maintenance components. What QM function leads to the update of the inspection intervals in the PM maintenance plan?

A. Defects Recording

B. Results Recording

C. Usage Decision

Short Answer: 113
Answer & Explanation: 135

13

Q-03:   A company asks that you identify the most
efficient means with which to record calibration
inspection results. How will you address that
requirement?

A. Results Recording Worklist

B. Results Recording

C. Usage Decision

Short Answer: 113
Answer & Explanation: 136

Q-04:   A company asks you to determine if each
piece of test equipment that is specified in a
maintenance order meets its predefined performance
specifications. How will you meet this requirement?

A. Process a calibration inspection using a
    maintenance task list

B. Process a calibration inspection using an inspection
    plan

C. Process a calibration inspection using a material
    specification

Short Answer: 113
Answer & Explanation: 136

Q-05:   A customer asks you to ensure that each
inspection point is valuated when the results of a
calibration inspection are recorded. How will you

adhere to this requirement using inspection point-related data in the planning objects? Select all that apply.

A. Select the "inspection points based on equipment" inspection point type in the task list header

B. Use the manual or automatic control indicator at the characteristic level of the maintenance task list

C. Select the "inspection points based on the inspection lot quantity" control indicator in the sampling procedure assigned to the task list characteristic

D. Select the "inspection points based on the inspection lot quantity" control indicator in the task list operation

E. Select the "inspection points based on the inspection lot quantity" inspection point type in the task list header

Short Answer: 113
Answer & Explanation: 137

Q-06:   The customer asks that information be documented regarding critical, abnormal properties of test equipment that are confirmed during a calibration inspection. How will you meet this requirement?

A. Create a notification item to address the critical damage to or defect in a piece of test equipment that is identified during the inspection

B. Create a defect record to document the critical damage to or defect in a piece of test equipment that is identified during the inspection

C. Use the inspection lot to document critical damage to or defect in a piece of test equipment that is identified during a calibration inspection

Short Answer: 113
Answer & Explanation: 138

Q-07:   A customer wants to document inspection results, generate inspection specifications for a piece of test equipment, confirm the quantity of equipment to be inspected and identify any inspection characteristic that must be inspected multiple times. How will you meet this customer requirement?

A. Create an inspection lot data record and document the required information in the record

B. Create an equipment master record and document the required information in the master record

C. Create a maintenance order and document the required information in the maintenance order

Short Answer: 113
Answer & Explanation: 139

Q-08: The customer wants to valuate each characteristic of a piece of test equipment as well as the piece of equipment itself on the basis of inspection results that are documented during a calibration inspection. How will you meet this customer requirement? Select all that apply.

A. Inspection results for each characteristic are documented at the operation level of the task list

B. Each characteristic of the test equipment and the test equipment itself is valuated on the basis of the recorded inspection results and valuation rules

C. The valuation of each characteristic and each piece of equipment is performed using a manual or automatic Results Recording function

Short Answer: 114
Answer & Explanation: 139

Q-09: The customer wants any critical defect in or damage to a piece of test equipment to be addressed as quickly as possible. How will you meet this requirement?

A. Use a manual procedure to record an outstanding notification to address the defect or damage during the defects recording process

B. Use an automated procedure to activate an outstanding notification to efficiently address the defect or damage

C. Use an automated process to record an outstanding maintenance notification item to address the defect or damage

D. Use a manual procedure to activate a maintenance notification item to efficiently address the defect or damage

Short Answer: 114
Answer & Explanation: 140

Q-10:   Some pieces of a company's test equipment fail shortly after the completion of a calibration inspection. The company uses a manual process, rather than an IT-based process, to track the inspections that were conducted using the test equipment and to identify and resolve any quality issues that may not have been identified during an inspection due to the use of the faulty test equipment. What QM report would you recommend to improve this process to more efficiently resolve quality issues? Select all that apply.

A. Defect Tracking Report

B. Test Equipment Tracking Report

C. Notification Tracking Report

Short Answer: 114
Answer & Explanation: 140

Q-11:   The customer requires the ability to analyze any documented critical damage to or defect in test equipment in terms of both its possible cause and solution. How can this requirement be met?

A. Activate an outstanding notification

B. Create a defect record

C. Create a maintenance order

Short Answer: 114
Answer & Explanation: 141

Q-12:   An inspection lot is created for a calibration inspection and the inspection characteristics are determined. Repeat measurements are to be documented for the characteristics. Which of the following triggers the repeat measurements?

A. Sampling procedure

B. Inspection instruction

C. Inspection characteristic

Short Answer: 114
Answer & Explanation: 142

Q-13:   A customer asks that you provide an inspector with specific information regarding the operations that are subject to a calibration inspection, the characteristics of the test equipment that are to be evaluated, as well as the inspection specifications for each characteristic. How can you accomplish this objective?

A. Create an inspection instruction and trigger its printout by means of an inspection lot control indicator

B. Create an inspection instruction and trigger its printout by means of a material master record control indicator

C. Create an inspection instruction and trigger its printout by means of the calculation of a sample size

Short Answer: 114
Answer & Explanation: 142

Q-14:   A customer asks that a piece of test equipment be classified as "not released for use" if a calibration inspection determines that the equipment does not meet its defined performance specifications. How can this objective be accomplished?

A. Update the equipment status in the equipment master record on the basis of the usage decision code that is entered for the inspection lot following a calibration inspection

B. Set the blocking indicator in the equipment master record on the basis of the usage decision code that is entered for the inspection lot following a calibration inspection

C. Set the deletion flag in the equipment master record on the basis of the usage decision code that is entered for the inspection lot following a calibration inspection

Short Answer: 114
Answer & Explanation: 143

Q-15:   The customer requires the ability to revise a maintenance inspection interval irrespective of previous inspection results. How can you accomplish this objective?

A. Change the cycle modification factor in the maintenance plan as the usage decision is entered to shorten an inspection interval

B. Change the cycle modification factor in the equipment master record as the usage decision is entered to shorten an inspection interval

C. Change the cycle modification factor in the maintenance task list as the usage decision is entered to shorten an inspection interval

Short Answer: 114
Answer & Explanation: 143

Q-16:   The customer requires the ability to identify inspection lots that have been inspected using a particular piece of test equipment. This ability is required in the event that the test equipment fails subsequent to one inspection and prior to the next.

Should this occur, it may be necessary to review previous inspection results that were obtained through the use of this equipment to ensure the results were accurate. How can this objective be accomplished?

A. A usage list created with the Test Equipment Tracking function

B. A usage list created with the Results Recording function

C. A usage list created with the Usage Decision function

Short Answer: 115
Answer & Explanation: 144

Q-17:   A maintenance order is triggered by a maintenance plan. The release of the maintenance order triggers the creation of an inspection lot and the calculation of the inspection lot quantity. Which of the following objects determines the inspection lot quantity?

A. Maintenance order

B. Equipment master record

C. Sampling procedure

Short Answer: 115
Answer & Explanation: 145

Q-18:   What can be used to identify the test equipment that is due for a calibration inspection, which will determine if the equipment adheres to predefined performance specifications?

A. Maintenance order

B. Maintenance specification

C. Equipment master record

Short Answer: 115
Answer & Explanation: 145

Q-19:   Where is it possible to specify the inspection activities that are to be conducted by a quality inspector at a specific work center to evaluate the test equipment?

A. Inspection instruction

B. Inspection lot header

C. Inspection lot operation

Short Answer: 115
Answer & Explanation: 146

Q-20:   Where is it possible to document a description of the test equipment to be inspected at a particular work center, the characteristics to be inspected and the specifications for each inspection characteristic?

A. Inspection instruction

B. Inspection lot

C. Inspection operation

Short Answer: 115
Answer & Explanation: 147

Q-21:   Where is the inspection points control data for a calibration inspection maintained? Select all that apply.

A. Maintenance task list header

B. Maintenance task list operation

C. Sampling procedure

D. Maintenance task list characteristic

Short Answer: 115
Answer & Explanation: 147

Q-22:   Where is information documented that pertains to critical damage to or a defect in test equipment, which is identified during a calibration inspection, to ensure that the damage or defect is addressed by the appropriate business partner?

A. Notification item

B. Defect record

C. Inspection lot

Short Answer: 115
Answer & Explanation: 148

Q-23:   A maintenance order is triggered by a
maintenance plan. In turn, an inspection lot is created
and the inspection lot quantity is calculated. Which of
the following determines the inspection type?

A. Inspection type defined in the maintenance order

B. Inspection type defined in the maintenance plan

C. Inspection type defined in the maintenance strategy

Short Answer: 115
Answer & Explanation: 149

Q-24:   What function can you use to record items in
a maintenance notification that pertain to critical
defects that are identified during a calibration
inspection?

A. Results Recording

B. Create Maintenance Notification

C. Usage Decision

Short Answer: 115
Answer & Explanation: 149

Q-25:   An inspection lot is created and the inspection
characteristics are determined. In turn, repeat
measurements are defined for the characteristics. Which

of the listed parameters determines if it is possible to record repeat measurements for test equipment? Select all that apply.

A. Maintenance order

B. Inspection characteristic control key in inspection operation

C. Sampling procedure

Short Answer: 115
Answer & Explanation: 150

Q-26: What function can be used to analyze the origin of a recorded defect and implement an appropriate corrective action that will address the documented issue?

A. Maintenance Notification

B. Results Recording

C. Defects Recording

Short Answer: 115
Answer & Explanation: 151

Q-27: An inspection lot is created, the inspection is conducted and inspection characteristics are valuated. In addition, defects in and damage to the test equipment are documented in defect records and maintenance notifications. Which of the listed

parameters triggers the automatic creation of the
notification?

A. Assignment of maintenance notification type to
    calibration inspection type

B. Selection of the defects recording control indicator
    for the inspection characteristic

C. Assignment of defect class to defect code

Short Answer: 115
Answer & Explanation: 151

Q-28:   What function can be used to identify a lot
that was inspected with a particular piece of test
equipment?

A. Test Equipment Tracking Report

B. Display Maintenance Plan

C. Display Equipment Master Record

Short Answer: 115
Answer & Explanation: 152

Q-29:   What object do you use to conduct several
calibration inspections and document the characteristic
results of each within an operation?

A. Inspection point

B. Inspection lot

C. Inspection characteristic

Short Answer: 115
Answer & Explanation: 153

Q-30:   What object is used to trigger the creation of
an inspection lot data record with which to manage
both the inspection specification and the recorded
results for a calibration inspection?

A. Maintenance plan

B. Maintenance order

C. Equipment master record

Short Answer: 116
Answer & Explanation: 153

Q-31:   An inspection lot is created and both the
inspection characteristics and the inspection lot are
valuated. Measurements are recorded in measurement
documents for each measuring point defined for the
test equipment and the documents are included in the
equipment history. Which of the following triggers the
creation of the measurement documents? Select all that
apply.

A. Master inspection characteristics in maintenance
   task list and measuring point master records linked
   by class characteristics

B. Completion of maintenance order

C. Completion of all tasks planned for the maintenance order

Short Answer: 116
Answer & Explanation: 154

Q-32: Which of the following is used to analyze the origin of damage to or a defect in a piece of test equipment that is identified during a calibration inspection?

A. Maintenance notification

B. Defect record

C. Equipment master record

Short Answer: 116
Answer & Explanation: 155

Q-33: What function triggers the calculation of a quality score for an inspection lot?

A. Usage Decision

B. Results Recording

C. Defects Recording

Short Answer: 116
Answer & Explanation: 155

Q-34: Which of the following functions triggers the follow-up actions for a calibration inspection?

A. Usage Decision

B. Results Recording

C. Defects Recording

Short Answer: 116
Answer & Explanation: 156

Q-35:   What function triggers the update of the equipment status in an equipment master record?

A. Usage Decision

B. Results Recording

C. Defects Recording

Short Answer: 116
Answer & Explanation: 156

Q-36:   What leads to an update of a cycle modification factor, which determines the inspection interval for test equipment?

A. Usage decision code

B. Defect code

C. Characteristic value

Short Answer: 116
Answer & Explanation: 157

Q-37: What function triggers the update of measurement documents in which the results of a calibration inspection are recorded?

A. Usage Decision

B. Results Recording

C. Defects Recording

Short Answer: 116
Answer & Explanation: 158

Q-38: A company that conducts calibration inspections of test equipment has a problem with ensuring that corrective actions that address the origin of defects that are identified during the calibration inspections are initiated in a timely manner to. What is an argument for implementing the Test Equipment Management component to overcome this issue?

A. Maintenance notification item is recorded at the time a critical defect is recorded

B. Maintenance strategy is used to schedule periodic calibration inspections

C. Cycle modification factor can be updated when the usage decision is documented

D. Measurement documents are automatically created for each measuring point

Short Answer: 116
Answer & Explanation: 158

Q-39:   A company that conducts calibration inspections of test equipment has a problem with the consistent inspection of the equipment by individual inspectors. What are arguments for implementing the Test Equipment Management component to overcome this issue? Select all that apply.

A. The ability to create inspection instructions to describe the processes required to draw a sample and to conduct an inspection at a particular work center

B. The ability to create an inspection instruction to define the inspection specification for each characteristic

C. The ability to create inspection instruction that specifies the maintenance order number, material and inspection lot subject to an inspection

Short Answer: 116
Answer & Explanation: 159

Q-40:   A company that conducts calibration inspections of test equipment has a problem with the initiation of the inspections in a timely manner. What are arguments for implementing the Test Equipment Management component to overcome this problem? Select all that apply.

A. The ability to define the cycle modification factor for the maintenance plan

B. The ability to define preventive maintenance cycles in the maintenance plan

C. The ability to define test equipment master records to record a test equipment status that indicates the due date of the calibration inspection

Short Answer: 116
Answer & Explanation: 160

Q-41: A company that conducts calibration inspections has a problem with identifying the characteristics of test equipment that should be inspected on a repeat basis. What are arguments for implementing the Test Equipment Management component to overcome this issue?

A. Assignment of sampling procedures to inspection characteristics in the maintenance task list

B. Assignment of sampling procedures to the maintenance task list header

C. Assignment of the sampling procedure to the calibration inspection type

Short Answer: 117
Answer & Explanation: 160

Q-42: A company that conducts calibration inspections has a problem with the consistent valuation of inspected test equipment. What are arguments for the implementation of the Test Equipment Management component functionality to overcome this problem? Select all that apply.

A. Predefined specifications for inspection characteristics are defined in the maintenance task list

B. Automatic valuation of test equipment using the valuation mode that is set for an inspection point in the material task list

C. Automatic valuation of inspection characteristics when defects or damages are confirmed

Short Answer: 117
Answer & Explanation: 161

Q-43:   A company that conducts calibration inspections has problems with deploying an efficient means by which to record the results of a calibration inspection and take needed actions on the basis of the usage decision. Which of the following is a valid argument for the use of calibration inspection processing to overcome these problems? Select all that apply.

A. Automatic proposal of follow-up action per the usage decision code

B. Automatic proposal of follow-up action per the defect code

C. Automatic proposal of follow-up action per the characteristic valuation

Short Answer: 117
Answer & Explanation: 162

Q-44:   A company that conducts calibration inspections has problems with efficiently conducting the steps of a calibration inspection and valuating test equipment following the documentation of inspection results. What is an argument for implementing the Test Equipment Management component to overcome this problem?

A. Automatic creation of inspection lot

B. Automatic execution of follow-up actions

C. Automatic selection of characteristic specifications for inspection instructions

Short Answer: 117
Answer & Explanation: 163

Q-45:   A customer wants to repair items in-house instead of sending technicians on-site. What can you set up for the in-house repair order? Select all that apply.

A. Automatic creation of inspection lot for the maintenance order

B. Execution of maintenance notifications

C. Confirmation of time and parts directly in the Maintenance order

D. Individual master records for the specific pieces of test equipment

Short Answer: 117
Answer & Explanation: 163

Q-46: Your customer is using the QM calibration inspection functionality. During system testing, the inspection characteristics do not appear in the maintenance task list although the master inspection characteristics have been defined. What may be the issue?

A. Maintenance task list is not assigned to inspection lot

B. Inspection characteristics control indicator is not selected for the operation

C. Maintenance task list is not assigned to the order

Short Answer: 117
Answer & Explanation: 165

Q-47: A company that conducts calibration inspections has problems with effectively incorporating the results of the inspections into its planned maintenance activities. What is one argument for implementing the Test Equipment Management component to overcome these problems?

A. Usage decision follow-up action "change cycle modification factor" in the maintenance plan

B. Usage decision follow-up action "change cycle modification factor" in the equipment master record

C. Usage decision follow-up action "change cycle modification factor" in the inspection lot

Short Answer: 117
Answer & Explanation: 166

Q-48: A company that conducts calibration inspections has problems with preventing the use of test equipment that does not meet predefined specifications. What is one argument for implementing the Test Equipment Management component to overcome these problems?

A. Proposed equipment master record status update by means of the Usage Decision follow-up function

B. Automatic equipment master record status update by means of the Usage Decision follow-up function

C. Manual equipment master record status update by means of the Usage Decision follow-up function

Short Answer: 117
Answer & Explanation: 167

Q-49: A company that conducts calibration inspections has problems with ensuring that a test equipment maintenance schedule reflects the actual physical status of test equipment rather than the presumed physical status based on the equipment status in the equipment master record. What are arguments for implementing calibration inspections to overcome these problems? Select all that apply.

A. Cycle modification factor is defined in maintenance plan

B. Preventive maintenance cycles are defined in the maintenance plan

C. Test equipment status defined in the equipment master record to indicate the due date of the calibration inspection

Short Answer: 117
Answer & Explanation: 167

Q-50:   A company that conducts calibration inspections has problems with the timely completion of maintenance orders subsequent to the completion of maintenance inspection activities. What is an argument for implementing calibration inspection processing to overcome these problems?

A. Completion of the maintenance order on the basis of the inspection lot usage decision code

B. Completion of the maintenance order on the basis of the equipment status

C. Completion of the maintenance order on the basis of measurement documents

Short Answer: 118
Answer & Explanation: 168

Q-51:   A company that conducts calibration inspections has problems with identifying inspection lots that were inspected using test equipment that did not adhere to predefined performance specifications. What are arguments for implementing the Test Equipment Management component to overcome these problems? Select all that apply.

A. Test Equipment Tracking function

B. Test Equipment Usage List

C. Inspection Lot List

Short Answer: 118
Answer & Explanation: 169

Q-52:   A customer calls you with the problem that characteristic results were not recorded for inspection points during a calibration inspection. What could be the reason?

A. Inspection point type is not defined in the maintenance task list header

B. Inspection point valuation mode is not defined at the operation level

C. Inspection point control indicator is selected for the sampling procedure defined at the characteristic level of the maintenance task list

D. Inspection point valuation mode is not defined at the characteristic level

E. Inspection point type is not defined in the material master record

Short Answer: 118
Answer & Explanation: 169

Q-53: Your customer is using calibration inspection functionality. During the inspection, the inspection lot is not valuated although the inspection results for the calibration inspection are recorded in the inspection lot. What may be the reason?

A. Inspection points not defined in task list

B. The sampling procedure that is assigned to a characteristic includes valuation mode that requires a manual entry

C. Control key for operation does not specify inspection characteristics

Short Answer: 118
Answer & Explanation: 170

Q-54: A customer calls you with the problem that a maintenance notification item cannot be created during the results recording process of a calibration inspection. What could be the reason? Select all that apply.

A. The maintenance notification type is not assigned to the inspection type in Customizing

B. The defects recording control indicator for the inspection characteristic is not set

C. Defect class is not assigned to the defect code

Short Answer: 118
Answer & Explanation: 171

Q-55:   A customer notifies you that he is unable to enter a usage decision for an inspection lot during a calibration inspection. What could be the reason? Select all that apply.

A. A piece of equipment has not yet been valuated for an inspection operation

B. The customer does not have the authorization to enter the usage decision for the inspection lot

C. No active status exists for the inspection lot

Short Answer: 118
Answer & Explanation: 172

Q-56:   A customer calls you with the problem that the status of test equipment was not changed following a calibration inspection. What could be the reason?

A. The equipment type of the test equipment is not PRT-relevant

B. The usage decision code is not PRT-relevant

C. The inspection type is not PRT-relevant

Short Answer: 118
Answer & Explanation: 172

Q-57:   A customer calls you with the problem that a piece of test equipment failed shortly after it passed a calibration inspection. What could be the reason?

A. The cycle modification factor was not adjusted subsequent to the calibration inspection to shorten the inspection interval

B. The equipment status was not adjusted subsequent to the calibration inspection to shorten the inspection interval

C. The preventive maintenance cycle was not adjusted subsequent to the calibration inspection to shorten the inspection interval

Short Answer: 118
Answer & Explanation: 173

Q-58:   A customer calls you with the problem that measurement documents are not updated to reflect the results of the calibration inspection. What could be the reason?

A. The master inspection characteristics assigned to the maintenance task list are not linked to the measuring point master records by means of class characteristics

B. The appropriate usage decision follow-up action is not linked to the equipment results history

C. The equipment results history is blank

Short Answer: 119
Answer & Explanation: 174

Q-59: A customer calls you with the problem that it is not possible to determine what inspection characteristics were inspected by means of one particular piece of test equipment. What could be the reason? Select all that apply.

A. An equipment master record is not created for the piece of test equipment

B. The equipment is not identified as a production resource/tool in the task list operation

C. The test equipment is not assigned to the inspection characteristic

D. The work center field for the equipment master is defined as history-relevant

Short Answer: 119

Answer & Explanation: 174

Q-60:   Your customer is using the test equipment
management functionality for calibration inspection
processes. During testing, the dialog box with which to
record maintenance notification items does not appear
at the entry of a negative valuation of a characteristic
although the maintenance notification type has been
assigned to the calibration inspection type. What may
be the reason?

A. Inspection characteristics must be inspected more
than one time

B. Inspection type is not assigned to notification type

C. Defects recording control indicator is not set for
inspection operation

Short Answer: 119
Answer & Explanation: 175

Q-61:   Which of the following statements regarding a
calibration inspection is correct?

A. Measuring point master records and master
inspection characteristics must be linked by means
of class characteristics to create measurement
documents
B. Recording inspection results requires that the
inspection lot is created automatically on the basis
of an equipment master

44

C. Inspection results are entered for each required operation

Short Answer: 119
Answer & Explanation: 176

Q-62: When a maintenance notification is created with reference to a valuation of a characteristic of a material in an inspection lot, how is maintenance notification type determined?

A. Maintenance notification type control indicator is set for inspection characteristic

B. Maintenance notification type is defined in maintenance task list

C. Maintenance notification type is assigned to the calibration inspection type in Customizing

Short Answer: 119
Answer & Explanation: 177

Q-63: Which of the following criteria influence the notification type that is used to document damage to or defects in test equipment?

A. Assignment of maintenance notification type to task list type in IMG

B. Assignment of maintenance notification type to the calibration inspection type in the IMG

C. Assignment of maintenance notification type to the defect code in the IMG

Short Answer: 119
Answer & Explanation: 178

Q-64:   Which of the following items controls the selection of the valuation mode that is used to indicate if a piece of test equipment is accepted or rejected for its intended purpose according to calibration inspection results?

A. Maintenance task list

B. Inspection point

D. Sampling procedure

Short Answer: 119
Answer & Explanation: 179

Q-65:   Which of the following parameters controls the performance of repeat inspections during a calibration inspection?

A. Inspection instruction

B. Sampling procedure

C. Inspection characteristic

Short Answer: 119
Answer & Explanation: 179

Q-66: Which of the following criteria influences the conduct of a calibration inspection using inspection points? Select all that apply.

A. Entry of equipment inspection point type in the maintenance task list header

B. Entry of equipment inspection point type at the characteristic level of the maintenance task list

C. Entry of the sampling procedure at the characteristic level of the maintenance task list

D. Entry of the sampling procedure in the maintenance task list header

Short Answer: 119
Answer & Explanation: 180

Q-67: For what purpose do you use automatic follow-up functions for a usage decision during a calibration inspection? Select all that apply.

A. Update the status of the inspection lot

B. Update the inspection interval in the preventive maintenance plan

C. Create measurement documents to record the inspection results for measurement points

Short Answer: 120
Answer & Explanation: 180

Q-68: For which purpose is the status of test equipment updated following a calibration inspection?

A. Control the release of test equipment for future use on the basis of the results of previous calibration inspection

B. Control the creation of a maintenance notification item on the basis of the results of previous calibration inspection

C. Control the revision of a maintenance order on the basis of the results of previous calibration inspection

Short Answer: 120
Answer & Explanation: 181

Q-69: For which purpose do you use the "revise a cycle modification factor in a maintenance plan" follow-up action?

A. Control the time period between one calibration inspection and the next

B. Control the time period between the issuance of one maintenance order and the next

C. Control the time period between the creation of one measurement document and the next

Short Answer: 120
Answer & Explanation: 182

Q-70: For what purpose is a measurement document created in relation to a calibration inspection?

A. Document the results of a calibration inspection for an inspection characteristic

B. Document the results of a calibration inspection for an inspection lot

C. Document the results of a calibration inspection for an inspection point

Short Answer: 120
Answer & Explanation: 183

Q-71: For what purpose do you complete a maintenance order on a technical basis following a calibration inspection?
A. Denotes the completion of the planned activities for an inspection lot

B. Denotes the completion of the planned activities for a task list

C. Denotes the completion of the planned activities for a maintenance order

Short Answer: 120
Answer & Explanation: 183

Q-72: For what purpose do you track test equipment?

A. Identify inspection lots that were inspected using a particular piece of test equipment

B. Identify inspection characteristics that were inspected using a particular piece of test equipment

C. Identify inspection operations that were performed using a particular piece of test equipment

Short Answer: 120
Answer & Explanation: 184

Q-73:   Which transaction enables you to process more than one inspection lot simultaneously?

A. Results Recording Worklist

B. Usage Decision Worklist

C. Defects Recording Worklist

Short Answer: 120
Answer & Explanation: 184

Q-74:   Which function enables you to both record calibration inspection results and valuate each piece of equipment after the results are recorded? Select all that apply.

A. Results Recording Worklist

B. Manual Results Recording

C. Usage Decision

D. Automatic Results Recording

E. Defects Recording

Short Answer: 120
Answer & Explanation: 185

Q-75:   Which of the following enables you to use a manual process to record items in a maintenance notification?

A. Results Recording

B. Usage Decision

C. Defects Recording

D. Results Recording Worklist

Short Answer: 120
Answer & Explanation: 185

Q-76:   Which function enables you to calculate a quality score automatically?

A. Usage Decision

B. Results Recording

C. Results Recording Worklist

Short Answer: 120
Answer & Explanation: 186

Q-77: Which transaction triggers the update of the status of test equipment to reflect whether or not the equipment meets predefined performance specifications?

A. Usage Decision

B. Results Recording

C. Results Recording Worklist

D. Defects Recording

Short Answer: 120
Answer & Explanation: 186

Q-78: What transaction triggers a change in the cycle modification factor to revise the calibration inspection interval in a maintenance plan?

A. Usage Decision

B. Results Recording

C. Results Recording Worklist

D. Defects Recording

Short Answer: 121
Answer & Explanation: 187

Q-79: What transaction triggers the creation of measurement documents for each measurement point during a calibration inspection?

A. Usage Decision

B. Results Recording

C. Results Recording Worklist

D. Defects Recording

Short Answer: 121
Answer & Explanation: 188

Q-80: What transaction leads to the technical completion of a maintenance order that was originally used to trigger the creation of the inspection lot for the calibration inspection?

A. Usage Decision

B. Results Recording

C. Results Recording Worklist

D. Defects Recording

Short Answer: 121
Answer & Explanation: 188

Q-81: What function enables you to identify the inspection characteristics that were inspected with a particular piece of test equipment in the event a subsequent calibration inspection determines the equipment does not adhere to predefined performance specifications?

A. Test Equipment Tracking

B. Inspection Lot List

C. Equipment Master History

Short Answer: 121
Answer & Explanation: 189

Q-82: In what case should your customer work with calibration inspections?

A. A need exists to determine if a piece of equipment that is specified in a maintenance order meets a set of performance specifications

B. A need exists to determine if a piece of equipment that is specified in a maintenance plan meets a set of performance specifications

C. A need exists to determine if a piece of equipment that is specified in an inspection lot meets a set of performance specifications

Short Answer: 121
Answer & Explanation: 189

Q-83: What task list usage is selected for a maintenance task list?

A. Plant Maintenance

B. Quality Management

C. Test Equipment Management

Short Answer: 121
Answer & Explanation: 190

Q-84:   What notification category is selected for the documentation of issues with test equipment, which are identified during a calibration inspection?

A. Service notification

B. Maintenance notification

C. Quality notification

Short Answer: 121
Answer & Explanation: 190

Q-85:   In what case should your customer work with a maintenance notification? Select all that apply.

A. Document the existence of critical equipment defects that require analysis to determine a corrective action

B. Document the rejection of inspection characteristics during the Results Recording process

C. Document change in inspection lot to adhere to inspection specification

Short Answer: 121
Answer & Explanation: 191

Q-86:   In what case should your customer work with a usage decision follow-up function for a calibration inspection? Select all that apply.

A. Requirement for the update of the status of inspection lot

B. Requirement to shorten the equipment inspection interval

C. Requirement to create measurement documents for each measurement point

D. Complete maintenance order from a technical and business perspective

E. Calculate quality score for inspection lot

Short Answer: 121
Answer & Explanation: 192

Q-87:   What determines an inspection lot quantity for a calibration inspection?

A. Sampling procedure

B. Maintenance order

C. Maintenance specification

Short Answer: 121
Answer & Explanation: 193

Q-88:   What determines the inspection activities that are conducted at a particular work center?

A. Inspection lot operation

B. Sampling procedure

C. Inspection instruction

Short Answer: 121
Answer & Explanation: 193

Q-89:   T/F: Using inspection points, it is possible to inspect multiple pieces of test equipment and record the characteristic results within one operation of an inspection plan.

A. True

B. False

Short Answer: 121
Answer & Explanation: 194

Q-90:   T/F: It is possible to document a defective property of a piece of test equipment even if the related characteristic is not referenced in the inspection plan.

A. True

B. False

Short Answer: 122
Answer & Explanation: 194

Q-91:   What function is used to implement a
corrective action that will address a documented issue?

A. Results Recording

B. Defects Recording

C. Notifications

Short Answer: 122
Answer & Explanation: 195

Q-92:   T/F It is possible to require that a
characteristic be inspected more than one time during a
calibration inspection.

A. True

B. False

Short Answer: 122
Answer & Explanation: 195

Q-93:   T/F It is possible to trigger the calculation of
a quality score on the basis of a usage decision for an
inspection lot.

A. True

B. False

Short Answer: 122
Answer & Explanation: 196

Q-94:   It is possible to automatically restrict the future use of a piece of test equipment on the basis of the valuation of the equipment as a result of a calibration inspection.

A. True

B. False

Short Answer: 122
Answer & Explanation: 196

Q-95:   What determines a calibration inspection lot quantity?

A. Maintenance specification

B. Maintenance order

C. Maintenance task list

Short Answer: 122
Answer & Explanation: 197

Q-96:   It is possible to use an automatic process to complete a maintenance order that led to the creation of an inspection lot for a calibration inspection.
A. True

B. False

Short Answer: 122
Answer & Explanation: 197

Q-97:   Which of the following criteria determines that an inspection instruction for a calibration inspection is printed automatically at the creation of an inspection lot?

A.   Creation of inspection lot

B.   Calculation of sample size

C.   Specification of inspection point type

Short Answer: 122
Answer & Explanation: 198

Q-98:   Which of the following data elements are used in an inspection instruction for a calibration inspection? Select all that apply.

A.   Characteristic specification

B.   Inspection date

C.   Inspection type

D.   Material

Short Answer: 122
Answer & Explanation: 199

Q-99:   What objects are used to plan a calibration inspection with inspection points? Select all that apply.

A. Sampling procedure

B. Maintenance task list

C. Inspection point type

Short Answer: 122
Answer & Explanation: 199

Q-100:   What settings are used to enable the creation of a maintenance notification item? Select all that apply.

A. Assignment of maintenance notification type to the calibration inspection type in the task list header

B. Selection of defects recording control indicator in the inspection characteristic

C. Assignment of the defect class to the notification type in the IMG

Short Answer: 122
Answer & Explanation: 200

Q-101:   Your customer wants to plan a calibration inspection. How is the inspection point control data maintained in planning objects? Select all that apply.

A. The inspection point type is maintained in the maintenance task list header

B. The automatic or manual valuation setting is maintained in the task list characteristic

C. The QM control indicator for inspection points based on the lot quantity is maintained in the sampling procedure

Short Answer: 122
Answer & Explanation: 201

Q-102:   Your customer wants to plan for the creation of an inspection lot for a calibration inspection and in doing so, require that some inspection characteristics be inspected more than one time. Where do you maintain this data?

A. Sampling procedure assigned to task list header

B. Sampling procedure assigned to characteristics in a maintenance task list

C. Sampling procedure assigned to task list operation

Short Answer: 123
Answer & Explanation: 201

Q-103:   Your customer wants to plan the documentation of damage to or defects in a piece of test equipment during the results recording process. Where do you maintain the settings that control this process?

A. Inspection type

B. Inspection characteristic

C. Task list header

D. Task list operation

Short Answer: 123
Answer & Explanation: 202

Q-104:   Your customer wants to document the status
of a piece of test equipment on the basis of the results
of a calibration inspection. Where do you maintain the
status data for the equipment?

A. Inspection lot

B. Equipment master record

C. Material master record

Short Answer: 123
Answer & Explanation: 203

Q-105:   Your customer wants to maintain inspection
intervals on the basis of the results of a calibration
inspection. Where do you maintain the cycle
modification factor?

A. Equipment master record

B. Maintenance task list

C. Maintenance plan

Q-106:   Your customer wants to plan inspection points for a calibration inspection. Where do you maintain the required inspection-point data?

A. Equipment master record

B. Maintenance task list

C. Inspection lot

D. Sampling procedure

E. Inspection type

Q-107:   Your customer wants to plan an equipment usage list with the Test Equipment Tracking function. Where do you maintain the necessary controls that enable this function? Select all that apply.

A. Print control indicator for equipment in inspection operation

B. Work center defined for inspection operation

C. Equipment defined for inspection characteristic

D. Equipment usage site defined in equipment master

Short Answer: 123
Answer & Explanation: 205

Q-108:   A maintenance order is triggered by a maintenance plan. An inspection lot is created and the inspection lot quantity is determined. Which of the following determines the inspection type?

A. Inspection type assigned to the inspection lot

B. Inspection type assigned to the maintenance order

C. Inspection type assigned to the maintenance plan

Short Answer: 123
Answer & Explanation: 205

Q-109:   During a calibration inspection, you find an incorrect inspection lot quantity. What do you check to identify the origin of the error in the number of pieces of equipment to be inspected?

A. Maintenance order

B. Inspection lot

C. Sampling procedure

Short Answer: 123
Answer & Explanation: 206

Q-110:   During a calibration inspection, you find that repeat measurements are performed incorrectly. Where do you check for the error in the repeat measurements?

A. Sampling procedure

B. Inspection characteristic

C. Task list header

Short Answer: 123
Answer & Explanation: 207

Q-111: Where is the test equipment status maintained? Select all that apply.

A. Material master record

B. Inspection lot

C. Equipment master record

Short Answer: 123
Answer & Explanation: 207

Q-112: A company runs both the Quality Management and Plant Maintenance solutions. Which transaction can be used to technically complete a maintenance order following a calibration inspection?

A. QM Usage Decision

B. QM Results Recording

C. QM Change Order

D. PM Change Order

66

Short Answer: 123
Answer & Explanation: 208

Q-113:   A company that conducts calibration inspections wants to ensure that identified critical defects in or damage to equipment are addressed. Which component do they need to implement to meet this objective?

A. Quality Planning

B. Notifications

C. Plant Maintenance

Short Answer: 123
Answer & Explanation: 208

Q-114:   A company conducts calibration inspections of test equipment to identify defects in or damage to the equipment. Which processes do they need to implement? Select all that apply.

A. Preventive Maintenance

B. Plant Maintenance

C. Maintenance Planning

D. Quality Planning

E. Classification System

Short Answer: 123

Answer & Explanation: 209

Q-115:   Which of the following is controlled by a
follow-up action that is executed subsequent to the
entry of the usage decision for test equipment? Select all
that apply.

A. Create measurement documents for each inspection
    point defined for the test equipment

B. Complete maintenance inspection on technical
    basis

C. Change cycle modification factor in maintenance
    task list

Short Answer: 124
Answer & Explanation: 210

Q-116:   Which of the following statements regarding
calibration inspection processing is correct?

A. A maintenance order is completed from a business
    standpoint following the entry of a usage decision
    for the inspection lot

B. A maintenance order is completed from a business
    standpoint following the technical completion of
    the calibration inspection

C. A maintenance order is completed from a business
    standpoint following the final posting of costs to
    the order

Short Answer: 124
Answer & Explanation: 210

Q-117:   A company that conducts calibration inspections wants to valuate equipment, calculate a quality score, and initiate other follow-up actions on the basis of inspection results. What function do they need to implement to perform the follow-up actions?

A. Results Recording

B. Usage Decision

C. Defects Recording

D. Results Recording Worklist

Short Answer: 124
Answer & Explanation: 211

Q-118:   A company is using the Test Equipment Management component. They need to conduct several inspections of test equipment, record characteristic results within an operation and valuate each inspection point automatically.   What is required to achieve this objective? Select all that apply.

A. Select the inspection points identifier based on inspection lot quantity in each sampling procedure assigned to the maintenance task list operation

B. Enter the inspection point type in the maintenance task list header

C. Select the inspection point valuation mode in the maintenance task list at the operation level

Short Answer: 124
Answer & Explanation: 212

Q-119:   A company is using the Test Equipment Management component. They need an inspection lot to be created automatically when a maintenance order is released. What Customizing activity is required to achieve this objective? Select all that apply.

A. Inspection type is assigned to the order type

B. Maintenance task list is assigned to the maintenance order

C. Inspection characteristics control indicator is selected for an inspection operation

Short Answer: 124
Answer & Explanation: 212

Q-120:   A company is using the Test Equipment Management component. They need to process several inspection lots simultaneously. What is required to achieve this objective?

A. Results Recording Worklist

B. Results Recording

C. Engineering Workbench

D. Usage Decision

E. Usage Decision Worklist

Short Answer: 124
Answer & Explanation: 213

Q-121:   A company is using the Test Equipment Management component. They need to promptly address critical defects in a piece of test equipment that are identified during the results recording process. What is required to achieve this objective? Select all that apply.

A. Notification type is assigned to the inspection type in Customizing

B. The defects recording control indicator is set in the inspection characteristics

C. Defect class is assigned to the usage decision catalog

Short Answer: 124
Answer & Explanation: 214

Q-122:   A company is using the Test Equipment Management component. They need to control the use of a piece of test equipment in inspections on the basis of the results of the calibration inspection of the test equipment. Which of the following is required to achieve this objective?

A. Equipment type is PRT-relevant

B. Notification type is assigned to the inspection type

C. Defects recording control indicator is set for inspection characteristic in inspection plan

Short Answer: 124
Answer & Explanation: 214

Q-123: A company is using the Test Equipment Management component. They need to revise the inspection intervals in a maintenance plan for test equipment on the basis of inspection results . What is required to achieve this objective? Select all that apply.

A. Function module for the follow-up function

B. Cycle modification factor

C. Equipment status

Short Answer: 124
Answer & Explanation: 215

Q-124: A company is using the Test Equipment Management component. The company requires the ability to record the results of a calibration inspection in measurement documents. What is required to achieve this objective? Select all that apply.

A. Measuring points defined for equipment

B. Linkage of measuring point master records to the master inspection characteristics in the maintenance task list

C. Measuring point master records defined in maintenance task list

D. Master inspection characteristics defined for measuring points

Short Answer: 124
Answer & Explanation: 216

Q-125: A customer is processing calibration inspections to determine if test equipment adheres to performance specifications. At what time during the calibration inspection process is the inspection lot for the calibration inspection created in the system?

A. Release of maintenance plan

B. Release of maintenance order

C. Scheduling of preventive maintenance

Short Answer: 124
Answer & Explanation: 216

Q-126: A customer is processing calibration inspections to determine if test equipment adheres to the related performance specifications. At what point during the calibration inspection process is the inspection instruction for the calibration inspection created in the system? Select all that apply.

A. Point that is determined by the user

B. Release of the maintenance order

C. Creation of the inspection lot

D. Calculation of sample size

Short Answer: 125
Answer & Explanation: 217

Q-127: A customer is processing calibration
inspections to determine if test equipment adheres to
the related performance specifications. At what time
during the calibration inspection process is a
maintenance notification created to analyze the origin
of a recorded defect and determine an appropriate
action to correct the defect? Select all that apply.

A. Defects recording process

B. Results recording process

C. Usage decision process

Short Answer: 125
Answer & Explanation: 217

Q-128: A customer is processing calibration
inspections to determine if test equipment adheres to
the related performance specifications. At what point
during the calibration inspection process is the status in
an equipment master updated to reflect the results of
the inspection?

A. Defects recording process

B. Results recording process

C. Usage decision process

Short Answer: 125
Answer & Explanation: 218

Q-129:   A customer is processing calibration inspections to determine if test equipment adheres to the related performance specifications. At what point during the calibration inspection process is the quality score for the inspection lot calculated?

A. Defects recording process

B. Results recording process

C. Usage decision process

Short Answer: 125
Answer & Explanation: 219

Q-130:   Which of the following statements relating to the calibration follow-up actions correct?

A.   Results Recording and Usage Decision functions can trigger follow-up function

B.   Calculate Quality Score is a follow-up action that can be performed using a dialog box

C. The current and proposed equipment status is displayed automatically following the entry of the usage decision

Short Answer: 125
Answer & Explanation: 219

Q-131:   A customer is processing calibration inspections to determine if test equipment adheres to the related performance specifications. At what point during the inspection process is the maintenance plan cycle modification factor adjusted for a piece of equipment that is accepted for its intended use following the inspection?

A. Defects recording process

B. Results recording process

C. Usage decision process

Short Answer: 125
Answer & Explanation: 220

Q-132:   What transaction allows you to record calibration results and valuate equipment?

A.   Usage Decision

B.   Results Recording Worklist

C.   Automatic Results Recording

Short Answer: 125

Answer & Explanation: 221

Q-133:   The customer wants to analyze damage to and defects in test equipment and to process corrective actions when necessary. Which function will fulfill this requirement?

A. Maintenance Notification

B. Test Equipment Tracking Report

C. Equipment Master History

Short Answer: 125
Answer & Explanation: 221

Q-134:   The customer wants to analyze the inspection lots, which include characteristics that were inspected with a particular piece of test equipment. How can this requirement be met?

A. Test Equipment Tracking Report

B. Equipment Master History

C. Maintenance Notification

Short Answer: 125
Answer & Explanation: 222

Q-135:   What manual transaction is used to record maintenance notification items?

A.   Results Recording

B.   Usage Decision

C.   Results Recording Worklist

Short Answer: 125
Answer & Explanation: 222

Q-136:   The Test Equipment Management component creates some calibration inspection lots automatically. How can you create additional inspection lots?

A. Create inspection lot using a manual process

B. Create and release a maintenance order using a manual process

C. Create and release maintenance plan

Short Answer: 125
Answer & Explanation: 223

Q-137:   The Test Equipment Management component can be used to record defect items and maintenance notification items automatically. How can you create a repair order?

A. Create inspection lot using a manual process which leads to the creation of a repair order

B. Create and release a repair order using an automatic process triggered by the maintenance notification item

C. Create and release a repair order using a manual process

Short Answer: 125
Answer & Explanation: 223

Q-138:   A customer asks about a solution to determine if each piece of test equipment used in a calibration inspection meets its predefined performance specifications. What component do you recommend?

A. Quality Management component

B. Test Equipment Management component

C. Plant Maintenance component

Short Answer: 125
Answer & Explanation: 224

Q-139:   A customer wants to streamline the calibration inspection process by recording inspection results for several inspection lots simultaneously. How can you achieve this objective ?

A. Function module

B. Results Recording Worklist function

C. Engineering Workbench

Short Answer: 125
Answer & Explanation: 224

Q-140:   The customer wants to reduce the effort required to identify and repair a defect that is discovered during a calibration inspection. What would you recommend? Select all that apply.

A. Trigger the creation of a maintenance notification on the basis of the defect code and defect class used to document the defect identified during the inspection

B. Trigger a repair order for the test equipment on the basis of the maintenance notification item

C. Trigger a repair order for the test equipment using the control indicator for the repair order in an inspection characteristic

Short Answer: 126
Answer & Explanation: 225

Q-141:   For what purpose is a usage decision follow-up function used?

A. Revise equipment inspection interval

B. Update status of inspection lot

C. Create measurement document for measuring point

Short Answer: 126
Answer & Explanation: 226

Q-142:   For what process is a worklist used in relation to a calibration inspection?

A. Defects Recording

B. Results Recording

C. Usage Decision

Short Answer: 126
Answer & Explanation: 226

Q-143:   For what purpose is a cycle modification factor used in relation to a calibration inspection?

A. Release of equipment for assignment to the inspection plan

B. Definition of inspection interval in maintenance plan

C. Documentation of calibration inspection results

D. Completion of maintenance order

Short Answer: 126
Answer & Explanation: 227

Q-144:   For what purpose is a measurement document used in relation to a calibration inspection?

A. Document inspection interval for preventive maintenance plan

B. Document acceptance or rejection of equipment for intended use

C. Document the results of a calibration inspection

Short Answer: 126
Answer & Explanation: 227

Q-145:   Your customer wants to display the use of test equipment at work centers. What do you recommend that they use?

A. Test Equipment Tracking Report

B. Equipment Master History

C. Plant Maintenance

Short Answer: 126
Answer & Explanation: 228

Q-146:   The customer wants to introduce the Test Equipment Management component to its users. What do you explain? Select all that apply.

A. Test Equipment Management is integrated with the Plant Maintenance components: Technical objects, and Preventive Maintenance and Plant Maintenance

B. The linkage between QM master data and the Classification system master data enables the synchronization of data between the systems

C. Create measuring points and create maintenance order are functions of the calibration inspection planning phase

Short Answer: 126
Answer & Explanation: 229

Q-147: Which of the following is a function of the inspection lot creation phase of a calibration inspection?

A. Create Maintenance Order

B. Change Cycle Modification Factor

C. Create Maintenance Task List

Short Answer: 126
Answer & Explanation: 229

Q-148: The cycle modification factor for a piece of test equipment specifies an inspection interval of 6 months in the maintenance plan. The equipment is inspected on 03/13/10 and is accepted for its intended use. The next inspection interval is 09/13/10. It is anticipated that the equipment will require maintenance on or around 05/10, which is well before the next scheduled inspection. What is a practical way to avoid the negative ramifications of the possible failure of the test equipment before the 09/13/10 date?

A. Shorten the inspection interval by changing the cycle modification factor

B. Change equipment status to "not released for use"

C. Increase the inspection interval by changing the cycle modification factor

D. Change equipment status to "released"

Short Answer: 126
Answer & Explanation: 230

Q-149:   Following a calibration inspection on 02/15/10, a piece of test equipment was determined to be not suitable for its intended use. The equipment was used in calibration inspections of material just prior to the February calibration inspection date. How can you avoid the negative ramifications of possible invalid inspection results based on the use of this test equipment?

A. Generate a test equipment tracking report that lists the use of a piece of test equipment at individual work centers as noted in the equipment usage list

B. Increase the inspection interval by changing the cycle modification factor

C. Change equipment status to "released"

Short Answer: 126
Answer & Explanation: 230

Q-150:   The maintenance order contains fields that have implications for the processing of a calibration inspection. If maintained on the maintenance order, a value will default onto subsequent records such as an inspection lot. The key that is assigned to the maintenance order that controls the generation of the inspection specifications for a particular combination of equipment and work center is referred to as what?

A. Maintenance task list

B. Equipment master record

C. Material master record

Short Answer: 127
Answer & Explanation: 231

Q-151:   The sampling procedure contains fields that have implications for the processing of multiple calibration inspections. If maintained for the sampling procedure, a value can default onto other records such as an inspection lot. The key that is assigned to the sampling procedure that identifies the pieces of equipment that are subject to the calibration inspection is referred to as what?

A. Inspection point

B. Equipment number

C. Measuring point

Short Answer: 127
Answer & Explanation: 232

Q-152:   The customer wants to record the results of a calibration inspection in measurement documents. What is required to do so?

A. Linkage of measuring point master records to the master inspection characteristics in the maintenance task list

B. Measuring point master records defined in maintenance task list

C. Measuring points defined for equipment

Short Answer: 127
Answer & Explanation: 232

Q-153: The maintenance task list contains fields that have implications for a calibration inspection. If maintained in the maintenance task list, a value will default to objects, such as an inspection lot. Which of the following is one such value that is specified in the maintenance task list that determines if an inspection characteristic is subject to repeat measurements?

A. Sampling procedure

B. Inspection point

C. Inspection type

Short Answer: 127
Answer & Explanation: 233

Q-154: The maintenance order contains fields that have implications for a calibration inspection. Which of the following is the key that is assigned to the maintenance order type that impacts the method used to record inspection results for test equipment?

A. Inspection type

B. Sampling procedure

C. Inspection point

Short Answer: 127
Answer & Explanation: 233

Q-155:   The maintenance task list contains fields that have implications for a calibration inspection. The key that is maintained in the maintenance task list that controls if defects identified during a calibration inspection are documented during a calibration inspection is referred to as what?

A. Defects recording control indicator in the inspection characteristic

B. Defect class defined for the defect code in the characteristic

C. Notification type in inspection operation

Short Answer: 127
Answer & Explanation: 234

Q-156:   What field is maintained in the task list characteristic that controls the creation of measurement documents in which the results of a calibration inspection are documented?

A. Class characteristic

B. Defect code

C. Notification type

Short Answer: 127
Answer & Explanation: 235

Q-157: The manner in which a calibration inspection
is conducted is dependent in part on the specification
of inspection points in the maintenance task list header.
If a calibration inspection calls for the use of inspection
points, the _____ must be set for
the task list.

A. Equipment or functional location inspection point
    type

B. Free inspection points during production inspection
    point type

C. Physical sample inspection point type

Short Answer: 127
Answer & Explanation: 236

Q-158: What is a prerequisite for the creation of an
inspection lot for a calibration inspection? Select all that
apply.

A. Assignment of plant maintenance inspection type to
    the maintenance order type

B. Assignment of inspection point type to
    maintenance item in order

C. Control key selected for inspection operation

Short Answer: 127
Answer & Explanation: 236

Q-159: What is a prerequisite for accepting or rejecting a characteristic during a calibration inspection? Select all that apply.

A. Definition of valuation mode for sampling procedure

B. Definition of sampling procedure in inspection characteristic

C. Definition of valuation mode for inspection characteristic

D. Definition of sampling procedure in inspection operation

Short Answer: 127
Answer & Explanation: 237

Q-160: What is a prerequisite for the creation of a maintenance notification item during a calibration inspection? Select all that apply.

A. Assignment of maintenance notification type to maintenance inspection type in Customizing

B. Assignment of notification type to inspection type in basic data

C. Defects recording control indicator in inspection characteristic

D. Defects recording control indicator in inspection operation

Short Answer: 128
Answer & Explanation: 238

Q-161: What is a prerequisite for the creation of an equipment usage list during a calibration inspection? Select all that apply.

A. Define equipment as PRT at the characteristic level of a task list

B. Assign test equipment to maintenance task list characteristic

C. Define work center in maintenance task list operation

D. Define test equipment usage in the work center field of the inspection characteristic

E. Create material master record for test equipment

Short Answer: 128
Answer & Explanation: 239

Q-162: A customer has planned calibration inspections for test equipment. How can you ensure that repeat measurements are performed for inspection characteristics?

A. Measuring points are defined for material master record

B. Sampling procedure is assigned to the maintenance task list characteristic

C. Link inspection characteristic in task list to measuring point master records by class characteristic

Short Answer: 128
Answer & Explanation: 240

Q-163:   A customer has planned calibration inspections for test equipment. How can he ensure that damage to or defects in test equipment is recorded for future review and management subsequent to the calibration inspection? Select all that apply.

A. Assignment of defect type to calibration inspection type

B. Assign maintenance notification type to calibration inspection type

C. Set the defects recording control indicator in the inspection characteristic

D. Set the defects recording control indicator in the inspection operation

Short Answer: 128
Answer & Explanation: 240

Q-164:   Which Plant Maintenance master data is required to conduct a calibration inspection?

A. Equipment master record

B. Sample drawing procedure

C. Master inspection characteristic

Short Answer: 128
Answer & Explanation: 241

Q-165: A customer wants to activate maintenance notification items during the calibration inspection process. What function makes this possible?

A. Usage Decision

B. Notification

C. Defects Recording

Short Answer: 128
Answer & Explanation: 242

Q-166:   A customer wants to record inspection activity times as calibration inspection results are recorded. What function makes this possible?

A. Usage Decision

B. Results Recording

C. Inspection Lot Completion

Short Answer: 128
Answer & Explanation: 242

Q-167: A customer wants to inspect some characteristics more than one time during a calibration inspection. How do you ensure this is possible?

A. Sampling procedure

B. Measuring point

C. Maintenance order

Short Answer: 128
Answer & Explanation: 243

Q-168: A customer wants a calibration inspection lot to be created automatically as a maintenance order is released. How do you ensure that this is possible? Select all that apply.

A. Assignment of calibration inspection type to maintenance order type

B. Assignment of maintenance task list to maintenance order

C. Assignment of inspection specification to inspection lot data record

D. Assignment of maintenance order to equipment master record

Short Answer: 128
Answer & Explanation: 244

Q-169: A customer wants to document damage to or defects in test equipment as calibration inspection results are recorded. How do you ensure this is possible? Select all that apply.

A. Assign the maintenance notification type to the calibration inspection type in the IMG

B. Select the defects recording control indicator for the inspection characteristic

C. Assign the maintenance notification type to the calibration inspection type in Basic Data

D. Select the defects recording control indicator for the inspection operation

Short Answer: 128
Answer & Explanation: 245

Q-170: A customer wants to process more than one inspection lot simultaneously. What transaction is used to do so?

A. Defects Recording Worklist

B. Usage Decision Worklist

C. Results Recording Worklist

Short Answer: 129
Answer & Explanation: 245

Q-171: A customer wants to implement a corrective action to address a documented issue. What transaction should be used to do so?

A. Results Recording

B. Defects Recording

C. Notifications

Short Answer: 129
Answer & Explanation: 246

Q-172: A customer conducts calibration inspections and relies on the Quality Management component to both plan and conduct the inspection. In addition, they want to resolve issues identified during the calibration inspection by means of maintenance orders and maintenance notifications. What component do you recommend for this purpose?

A. Quality Management

B. Plant Maintenance

C. Notifications

Short Answer: 129
Answer & Explanation: 246

Q-173:   What do you have to consider when you use
the Notifications component in combination with the
Test Equipment Management component? Select all
that apply.

A. Assignment of maintenance notification type to the
    calibration inspection type in the IMG

B. Entry of the defects recording control indicator in
    the inspection characteristic

C. Assignment of maintenance notification type to the
    calibration inspection type in the inspection lot

D. Entry of the defects recording control indicator in
    the maintenance task list header

Short Answer: 129
Answer & Explanation: 247

Q-174:   What do you have to consider when you use
measuring points in combination with the Test
Equipment Management component?

A. Link master inspection characteristics to measuring
    point master records by class characteristics

B. Link master inspection characteristics to a
    maintenance task list by class characteristics

C. Link master inspection characteristics to class
    characteristics by measuring point master records

Short Answer: 129

Q-175:   What do you have to consider when you use maintenance orders in combination with the Test Equipment Management component? Select all that apply.

A. Assignment of inspection points to characteristics

B. Assignment of calibration inspection type to maintenance order type

C. Assignment of maintenance task list to maintenance order

Short Answer: 129
Answer & Explanation: 249

Q-176:   What do you have to consider when you use inspection points in combination with the Test Equipment Management component? Select all that apply.

A. Define equipment inspection point type in maintenance task list header

B. Define automatic inspection point valuation mode

C. Select the inspection points control indicator in the maintenance task list characteristic

D. Select inspection points based on inspection lot quantity control indicator for sampling procedure

E. Define equipment inspection point type in maintenance order

Short Answer: 129
Answer & Explanation: 250

Q-177: A customer complains that the quantity of product in the inspection lot is incorrect. How can this error be corrected?

A. Correct the quantity in the maintenance task list

B. Correct the quantity in the inspection lot

C. Correct the quantity in the maintenance order

Short Answer: 129
Answer & Explanation: 251

Q-178: A customer complains about the valuation of test equipment following a calibration inspection. How can you address this complaint?

A. Change the valuation mode in the inspection type

B. Change the valuation mode in the maintenance task list

C. Change the valuation mode in the maintenance order

Short Answer: 130
Answer & Explanation: 251

Q-179: A customer complains about the failure of a piece of test equipment two months after the most recent calibration inspection but four months before the next scheduled inspection. How can you address this issue to prevent its reoccurrence of the issue?

A. Change the cycle modification factor in the equipment master record to implement a shorter inspection interval

B. Change the cycle modification factor in the maintenance plan to implement a shorter inspection interval

C. Change the cycle modification factor in the maintenance task list to implement a shorter inspection interval

Short Answer: 130
Answer & Explanation: 252

Q-180: A customer is using the Test Equipment Management component. Identify a setting that is required to plan a calibration inspection? Select all that apply.

A. Equipment type assigned to order type

B. Inspection points in maintenance order

C. Maintenance task list assigned to maintenance order

D. Master inspection characteristics control key for operation

E. Inspection points assigned to operation

Short Answer: 130
Answer & Explanation: 253

Q-181:   A customer is using the Test Equipment Management component. What function is required to create an inspection lot for a calibration inspection? Select all that apply.

A. Schedule preventive maintenance

B. Create maintenance task list

C. Change cycle modification factor

Short Answer: 130
Answer & Explanation: 254

Q-182:   A customer is using the Test Equipment Management component. What tasks must be performed to process a calibration inspection? Select all that apply.

A. Inspect test equipment

B. Make confirmation for a maintenance task list

C. Record inspection results

D. Create maintenance task list

E. Enter usage decision for inspection lot

Short Answer: 130
Answer & Explanation: 255

Q-183:   A customer would like to explore the option of using Calibration Inspection functionality. What are the main planning activities of the application that the customer should consider? Select all that apply.

A. Create material master record

B. Create measuring points

C. Create inspection characteristics

D. Define maintenance type

E. Create maintenance task list

F. Create preventive maintenance plan

Short Answer: 130
Answer & Explanation: 256

Q-184:   What are the main activities required to create an inspection lot for a calibration inspection? Select all that apply.

A. Schedule preventive maintenance

B. Create and release maintenance order

C. Create measuring points

D. Create mater inspection characteristic

Short Answer: 130
Answer & Explanation: 257

Q-185:   Identify a main calibration inspection processing activity. Select all that apply.

A. Inspect test equipment

B. Enter confirmation for maintenance order

C. Create maintenance task list

D. Define preventive maintenance strategy

Short Answer: 130
Answer & Explanation: 258

Q-186:   Employees often work on different inspections and the related appraisal costs must be posted to the appropriate project cost centers. What activity is used to ensure the appraisal costs are correctly assigned to the cost center?

A. Confirmations are made for maintenance orders

B. Operation assigned to order

C. Inspection type assigned to order type

Short Answer: 130

Answer & Explanation: 259

Q-187: Employees often conduct several inspections and record results within one inspection operation. Inspection results must be posted to the appropriate equipment and the test equipment must be valuated using the appropriate valuation rules. What object is used to ensure the inspection results are assigned to the appropriate equipment and that the equipment is accepted or rejected for future use on the appropriate basis?

A. Inspection point

B. Inspection lot

C. Maintenance task list

Short Answer: 130
Answer & Explanation: 260

Q-188: Employees often inspect a characteristic more than one time and record results within one inspection operation. Inspection results must be posted to the appropriate test equipment and the equipment must be valuated using the appropriate valuation rules. What basic data supports the performance of the repeat measurements?

A. Sampling procedure assigned to the characteristic

B. Inspection specifications in the inspection lot record

C. Quantity in maintenance order

Short Answer: 130
Answer & Explanation: 260

Q-189: Employees conduct calibration inspections and record damage to or defects in the test equipment that is inspected. Any recorded defect in or damage to the equipment must be analyzed to determine its cause and the solution to the issue. What ensures that any issue that led to the rejection of a piece of test equipment for its intended use is addressed and that the information that is documented in relation to the issue is appropriate for a calibration inspection? Select all that apply.

A. Assignment of maintenance notification type to calibration inspection type

B. Selection of the defects recording control indicator for the inspection characteristic

C. Assignment of inspection type to order type

Short Answer: 131
Answer & Explanation: 261

Q-190: Which of the following minimizes the efforts required to address a defect identified during a calibration inspection?

A. Creation of maintenance notification triggered by defect class

B. Creation of repair order triggered by notification item

C. Creation of repair order triggered by inspection characteristic

Short Answer: 131
Answer & Explanation: 262

Q-191:   Employees conduct calibration inspections to ensure that test equipment used in quality inspections adhere to prescribed performance criteria. During this process, calibration inspection results must be posted to the appropriate equipment and the equipment must be valuated using the appropriate valuation rules. However, it is not unusual for test equipment that is judged to meet performance criteria in one inspection to fail prior to the next regularly scheduled inspection. What key field is used to best ensure that the equipment that is accepted for future use on the basis of the current inspection results does not fail prior to the next subsequent scheduled inspection?

A. Cycle modification factor in the preventive maintenance plan

B. Cycle modification factor in the equipment master record

C. Cycle modification factor in the maintenance order

Short Answer: 131
Answer & Explanation: 262

Q-192:   A company is using the Test Equipment Management component. They need to determine the inspection characteristics that were evaluated with a particular piece of test equipment. What is required to achieve this objective? Select all that apply.

A. The test equipment is designated a production resource/tool at the task list operation level

B. The test equipment is assigned to an inspection operation

C. Equipment master records have been defined for the test equipment

D. The work center is defined at the task list characteristic level

Short Answer: 131
Answer & Explanation: 263

Q-193:   What components are directly integrated with the Test Equipment Management component? Select all that apply.

A. QM Technical Objects

B. PM Preventive Maintenance

C. PP Maintenance Processing

D. Classification System

Short Answer: 131

Q-194:   Which of the following is a standard calibration inspection usage decision entry method? Select all that apply.

A. Manual entry of the usage decision code for one single inspection lot

B. Manual entry of the usage decision code for more than one single inspection lot with the work list function

C. Automatic entry of the usage decision code for one single inspection lot

D. Automatic entry of the usage decision code for more than one single inspection lot

Short Answer: 131
Answer & Explanation: 264

Q-195:   Which of the following is a standard calibration inspection usage decision follow-up action?

A. Manual or proposed entry of the test equipment status

B. Manual or automatic creation of notification item

C. Manual or automatic creation of measurement documents

D. Manual or automatic technical completion of a maintenance task list

Short Answer: 131
Answer & Explanation: 266

Q-196:   What allows a customer to adapt an inspection schedule to most accurately reflect the actual usage of a piece of test equipment and its probable status and to prevent all out failure of the equipment while the equipment is in use?

  A. Cycle modification factor

  B. Inspection instruction

  C. Inspection point

Short Answer: 132
Answer & Explanation: 266

Q-197:   A customer considers implementing the Test Equipment Management component. Which of the following is a benefit of the component?

A. Master record maintained for the individual piece of test equipment

B. Support for the periodic calibration of test equipment

C. Creation of maintenance orders

D. Test equipment history is maintained for PRT

Short Answer: 132
Answer & Explanation: 267

Q-198: A company asks for a real-time report with which to analyze characteristics that were inspected with a specific piece of test equipment. The report should be formatted by inspection lot, characteristic and test equipment. What report can provide this information?

A. Test Equipment Tracking Report

B. Defects Tracking Report

C. Display Equipment Master Record

Short Answer: 132
Answer & Explanation: 268

Q-199: A company runs the Quality Management and Plant Maintenance components. What QM function posts activity times to PM maintenance orders? Select all that apply.

A. Defects Recording

B. Results Recording

C. Usage Decision

Short Answer: 132
Answer & Explanation: 268

Q-200:   A company runs the Quality Management and Plant Maintenance components. Which QM transaction posts the status of a piece of test equipment to PM equipment master records?

A. Defects Recording

B. Results Recording

C. Usage Decision

Short Answer: 132
Answer & Explanation: 269

Q-201:   What master record type is used for the definition and management of test equipment?

A. PRT master record

B. Equipment master record

C. Material master record

Short Answer: 132
Answer & Explanation: 270

CHAPTER II

SHORT ANSWERS

SHORT ANSWERS

Q-01:   B. The implementation of the QM Quality Planning and Test Equipment Management components and C. The implementation of the Classification System component

Q-02:   C. Usage Decision

Q-03:   A. Results Recording Worklist

Q-04:   A. Process a calibration inspection using a maintenance task list

Q-05:   A. Select the " inspection points based on equipment" inspection point type in the task list header and C. Select the "inspection points based on the inspection lot quantity" control indicator in the sampling procedure assigned to the task list characteristic

Q-06:   B. Create a defect record to document the critical damage to or defect in a piece of test equipment that is identified during the inspection

Q-07:   A. Create an inspection lot data record and document the required information in the record

Q-08:   B. Each characteristic of the test equipment and the test equipment itself is valuated on the basis of the recorded inspection results and valuation rules and C. The valuation of each characteristic and each piece of equipment is performed using a manual or automatic Results Recording function

Q-09:   B. Use an automated procedure to activate an outstanding notification to efficiently address the defect or damage

Q-10:   B. Test Equipment Tracking Report

Q-11:   A. Activate an outstanding notification

Q-12:   A. Sampling procedure

Q-13:   C. Create an inspection instruction and trigger its printout by means of the calculation of a sample size

Q-14:   A. Update the equipment status in the equipment master record on the basis of the usage decision code that is entered for the inspection lot following a calibration inspection

Q-15:   A. Change the cycle modification factor in the maintenance plan as the usage decision is entered to shorten an inspection interval

Q-16:   A. A usage list created with the Test Equipment Tracking function

Q-17:   A. Maintenance order

Q-18:   A. Maintenance order

Q-19:   A. Inspection instruction

Q-20:   A. Inspection instruction

Q-21:   A. Maintenance task list header, B. Maintenance task list operation and C. Sampling procedure

Q-22:   A. Notification item

Q-23:   B. Inspection type defined in the maintenance plan

Q-24:   A. Results Recording

Q-25:   A. Maintenance order and B. Inspection characteristic control key in inspection operation

Q-26:   A. Maintenance Notification

Q-27:   C. Assignment of defect class to defect code

Q-28:   A. Test Equipment Tracking Report

Q-29:   A. Inspection point

Q-30:   B. Maintenance order

Q-31:   A. Master inspection characteristics in
        maintenance task list and measuring point
        master records linked by class characteristics

Q-32:   A. Maintenance notification

Q-33:   A. Usage Decision

Q-34:   A. Usage Decision

Q-35:   A. Usage Decision

Q-36:   A. Usage Decision code

Q-37:   A. Usage Decision

Q-38:   A. Maintenance notification item is recorded
        at the time a critical defect is recorded

Q-39:   A. The ability to create inspection instructions
        to describe the processes required to draw a
        sample and conduct an inspection at a
        particular work center and B. The ability to
        create an inspection instruction to define the
        inspection specification for each characteristic

Q-40:   A. The ability to define the cycle modification
        factor for the maintenance plan and B. The
        ability to define preventive maintenance cycles
        in the maintenance plan

Q-41: A. Assignment of sampling procedures to inspection characteristics in the master task list

Q-42: A. Predefined specifications for inspection characteristics are defined in the maintenance task list and B. Automatic valuation of test equipment using the valuation mode that is set for an inspection point in the material task list

Q-43: A. Automatic proposal of follow-up action per the usage decision code

Q-44: A. Automatic creation of inspection lot and B. Automatic execution of follow-up actions

Q-45: A. Automatic creation of inspection lot for maintenance order

Q-46: B. Inspection characteristics control indicator is not selected for the operation

Q-47: A. Usage decision follow-up action "change cycle modification factor" in the maintenance plan

Q-48: A. Proposed equipment master record status update by means of the Usage Decision follow-up function

Q-49: A. Cycle modification factor is defined in maintenance plan

Q-50:   A. Completion of the maintenance order on the basis of the inspection lot usage decision code

Q-51:   A. Test Equipment Tracking function and B. Test Equipment Usage list

Q-52:   A. Inspection point type is not defined in the maintenance task list header and B. Inspection point valuation mode is not defined at the operation level

Q-53:   B. The sampling procedure that is assigned to a characteristic includes valuation mode that requires a manual entry

Q-54:   A. The maintenance notification type is not assigned to the inspection type in Customizing and B. The defects recording control indicator for the inspection characteristic is not set

Q-55:   A. A piece of equipment has not yet been valuated for an inspection operation and B. The customer does not have the authorization to enter the usage decision for the inspection lot

Q-56:   A. The equipment type of the test equipment is not PRT-relevant

Q-57:   A. The cycle modification factor was not adjusted subsequent to the calibration inspection to shorten the inspection interval

Q-58:   A. The master inspection characteristics
        assigned to the maintenance task list are not
        linked to the measuring point master records
        by means of class characteristics

Q-59:   B. The equipment is not identified as a
        production resource/tool in the task list
        operation and C. The test equipment is not
        assigned to the inspection characteristic

Q-60:   B. Inspection type is not assigned to
        notification type

Q-61:   **A. Measuring point master records and master
        inspection characteristics must be linked by
        means of class characteristics to create
        measurement documents**

Q-62:   C. Maintenance notification type is assigned to
        the calibration inspection type in Customizing

Q-63:   B. Assignment of maintenance notification
        type to the calibration inspection type in the
        IMG

Q-64:   C. Sampling procedure

Q-65:   B. Sampling procedure

Q-66:   A. Entry of equipment inspection point type
        in the maintenance task list header and C.
        Entry of the sampling procedure at the
        characteristic level of the maintenance task list

119

Q-67: B. Update the inspection interval in the preventive maintenance plan and C. Create measurement documents to record the inspection results for measurement points

Q-68: A. Control the release of test equipment for future use on the basis of the results of previous calibration inspection

Q-69: A. Control the time period between one calibration inspection and the next

Q-70: C. Document the results of a calibration inspection for an inspection point

Q-71: C. Denotes the completion of the planned activities for a maintenance order

Q-72: B. Identify inspection characteristics that were inspected using a particular piece of test equipment

Q-73: A. Results Recording Worklist

Q-74: A. Results Recording Worklist, B. Manual Results Recording and C. Usage Decision

Q-75: A. Results Recording

Q-76: A. Usage Decision

Q-77: A. Usage Decision

Q-78:   A. Usage Decision

Q-79:   A. Usage Decision

Q-80:   A. Usage Decision

Q-81:   A. Test Equipment Tracking

Q-82:   A. A need exists to determine if a piece of
equipment that is specified in a maintenance
order meets a set of performance specifications
and C. A need exists to determine if a piece of
equipment that is specified in an inspection lot
meets a set of performance specifications

Q-83:   A. Plant Maintenance

Q-84:   B. Maintenance notification

Q-85:   A. Document the existence of critical
equipment defects that require analysis to
determine a corrective action

Q-86:   B. Requirement to shorten the equipment
inspection interval and C. Requirement to
create measurement documents for each
measurement point

Q-87:   B. Maintenance order

Q-88:   C. Inspection instruction

Q-89:   A. True

Q-90:   A. True

Q-91:   C. Notifications

Q-92:   A. True

Q-93:   A. True

Q-94:   A. True

Q-95:   B. Maintenance order

Q-96:   A. True

Q-97:   B. Calculation of sample size

Q-98:   A. Characteristic specification and B. Inspection date

Q-99:   A. Sampling procedure and B. Maintenance task list

Q-100: A. Assignment of maintenance notification type to the calibration inspection type in the task list header and B. Selection of defects recording control indicator in the inspection characteristic

Q-101: A. The inspection point type is maintained in the maintenance task list header and C. The QM control indicator for inspection points based on the lot quantity is maintained in the sampling procedure

Q-102: A. Sampling procedure assigned to characteristics in a maintenance task list

Q-103: A. Inspection type and B. Inspection characteristic

Q-104: B. Equipment master record

Q-105: C. Maintenance plan

Q-106: B. Maintenance task list and C. Sampling procedure

Q-107: C. Equipment defined for inspection characteristic

Q-108: B. Inspection type assigned to the maintenance order

Q-109: A. Maintenance order

Q-110: A. Sampling procedure

Q-111: C. Equipment master record

Q-112: C. QM Change Order

Q-113: B. Notifications

Q-114: A. Preventive Maintenance, B. Plant Maintenance and D. Quality Planning

Q-115: A. Create measurement documents for each inspection point defined for the test equipment

Q-116: C. A maintenance order is completed from a business standpoint following the final posting of costs to the order

Q-117: B. Usage Decision

Q-118: B. Enter the inspection point type in the maintenance task list header

Q-119: A. Inspection type is assigned to the order type

Q-120: A. Results Recording Worklist

Q-121: A. Notification type is assigned to the inspection type in Customizing and B. The defects recording control indicator is set in the inspection characteristics

Q-122: A. Equipment type is PRT-relevant

Q-123: B. Cycle modification factor

Q-124: A. Measuring points defined for equipment and B. Linkage of measuring point master records to the master inspection characteristics in the maintenance task list

Q-125: B. Release of the maintenance order

Q-126: A. Point that is determined by the user and C. Creation of the inspection lot

Q-127: A. Defects recording process and B. Results recording process

Q-128: C. Usage decision process

Q-129: C. Usage decision process

Q-130: A. Results Recording and Usage Decision functions can trigger follow-up functions

Q-131: C. Usage decision process

Q-132: B. Results Recording Worklist

Q-133: A. Maintenance Notification

Q-134: A. Test Equipment Tracking Report

Q-135: A. Results Recording

Q-136: B. Create and release a maintenance order using a manual process

Q-137: B. Create and release a repair order using an automatic process triggered by the maintenance notification item

Q-138: B. Test Equipment Management component

Q-139: B. Results Recording Worklist function

Q-140: A. Trigger the creation of a maintenance notification on the basis of the defect code and defect class used to document the defect identified during the inspection

Q-141: A. Revise equipment inspection interval

Q-142: B. Results Recording

Q-143: B. Definition of inspection interval in maintenance plan

Q-144: C. Document the results of calibration inspection

Q-145: A. Test Equipment Tracking Report

Q-146: A. Test Equipment Management is integrated with the Plant Maintenance components: Technical objects, Preventive Maintenance and Plant Maintenance and B. The linkage between QM master data and the Classification system master data enables the synchronization of data between the systems

Q-147: A. Create Maintenance Order and C. Create Maintenance Task List

Q-148: A. Shorten the inspection interval by changing the cycle modification factor

Q-149: A. Generate a test equipment tracking report that lists the use of a piece of test equipment at individual work centers as noted in the equipment usage list

Q-150: A. Maintenance task list

Q-151: A. Inspection point

Q-152: A. Linkage of measuring point master records to the master inspection characteristics in the maintenance task list and C. Measuring points defined for equipment

Q-153: A. Sampling procedure

Q-154: A. Inspection type

Q-155: A. Defects recording control indicator in the inspection characteristic

Q-156: A. Class characteristic

Q-157: A. Equipment or functional location inspection point type

Q-158: A. Assignment of plant maintenance inspection type to the maintenance order type

Q-159: A. Definition of valuation mode for sampling procedure and B. Definition of sampling procedure in inspection characteristic

Q-160: A. Assignment of maintenance notification type to maintenance inspection type in Customizing and C. Defects recording control indicator in inspection characteristic

Q-161: B. Assign test equipment to maintenance task list characteristic and C. Define work center in maintenance task list operation

Q-162: B. Sampling procedure is assigned to the maintenance task list characteristic and C. Link inspection characteristic in task list to measuring point master records by class characteristic

Q-163: B. Assign maintenance notification type to calibration inspection type and C. Set the defects recording control indicator in the inspection characteristic

Q-164: A. Equipment master record

Q-165: A. Usage Decision

Q-166: A. Usage Decision

Q-167: A. Sampling procedure

Q-168: A. Assignment of calibration inspection type to maintenance order type

Q-169: A. Assign the maintenance notification type to the calibration inspection type in the IMG and

B. Select the defects recording control indicator for the inspection characteristic

Q-170:   C. Results Recording Worklist

Q-171:   C. Notifications

Q-172:   B. Plant Maintenance

Q-173:   A. Assignment of maintenance notification type to the calibration inspection type in the IMG and B. Entry of the defects recording control indicator in the inspection characteristic

Q-174:   A. Link master inspection characteristics to the measuring point master records by class characteristics

Q-175:   B. Assignment of calibration inspection type to maintenance order type and C. Assignment of maintenance task list to maintenance order

Q-176:   A. Define equipment inspection point type in maintenance task list header, B. Define automatic inspection point valuation mode and D. Select the inspection points based on inspection lot quantity control indicator for sampling procedure

Q-177:   C. Correct the quantity in the maintenance order

Q-178:   B. Change the valuation mode in the
         maintenance task list

Q-179:   B. Change the cycle modification factor in the
         maintenance plan to reflect a shorter
         inspection interval

Q- 180: C. Maintenance task list assigned to
         maintenance order and E. Inspection points
         assigned to operation

Q- 181: C. Create maintenance task list

Q-182:   A. Inspect test equipment, C. Record
         inspection results and E. Enter usage decision
         for inspection lot

Q-183:   B. Create measuring points and F. Create
         preventive maintenance plan

Q-184:   A. Schedule preventive maintenance and B.
         Create and release maintenance order

Q-185:   A. Inspect test equipment and B. Enter
         confirmation for maintenance order

Q-186:   A. Confirmations are made for maintenance
         orders

Q-187:   A. Inspection point

Q-188:   A. Sampling procedure assigned to the
         characteristic

Q-189: A. Assignment of maintenance notification type to calibration inspection type and B. Selection of the defects recording control indicator for the inspection characteristic

Q-190: A. Creation of maintenance notification triggered by defect class and B. Creation of repair order triggered by notification item

Q-191: A. Cycle modification factor in the preventive maintenance plan

Q-192: A. The test equipment is designated a production resource tool at the task list operation level and C. Equipment master records have been defined for the test equipment

Q-193: B. PM Preventive Maintenance and D. Classification System

Q-194: A. Manual entry of the usage decision code for one single inspection lot, B. Manual entry of the usage decision code for more than one single inspection lot with the work list function, C. Automatic entry of the usage decision code for one single inspection lot and D. Automatic entry of the usage decision code for more than one single inspection lot

Q-195: A. Manual or proposed entry of the test equipment status and C. Manual or automatic creation of measurement documents

Q-196: A. Cycle modification factor

Q-197: A. Master record maintained for the individual piece of test equipment and B. Support for the periodic calibration of test equipment

Q-198: A. Test Equipment Tracking Report

Q-199: A. Defects Recording, B. Results Recording and C. Usage Decision

Q-200: C. Usage Decision

Q-201: B. Equipment master record

CHAPTER III

ANSWERS & EXPLANATIONS

ANSWERS & EXPLANATIONS

Q-01:   B. The implementation of the QM Quality Planning and Test Equipment Management components and C. The implementation of the Classification System component.

The functional integration of a business is mirrored in the integration of the Test Equipment Management functions with those of the Quality Management and Plant Maintenance components, each of which support the conduct of calibration inspections. Such components include the PM Technical Objects, Preventive Maintenance and Maintenance Processing components, the QM Quality Planning and Test Equipment Management components and the Classification System component.

Q-02:   C. Usage Decision

A PM maintenance plan is the central planning object for a calibration inspection. The maintenance plan controls the type and scope of inspection activities to be performed and whether the activities are performed on a time or performance-basis. The cycle modification factor is an element of the maintenance plan that is used to alter a plan's time-based or performance-based maintenance cycle to best reflect the actual condition and maintenance requirements of a piece of test equipment. The inspection interval must be revised if the test equipment status, which is documented in the equipment master record, does not reflect the actual condition of the test equipment and if the equipment may require maintenance prior to the next scheduled inspection. In this instance, to preclude the possibility that the equipment may fail prior to the next subsequent inspection, the cycle modification factor in the maintenance plan is changed to reduce the inspection interval as the inspection lot usage decision is documented.

Q-03:   A. Results Recording Worklist

After the inspection of a piece of test equipment, the inspection results for the individual characteristics that are defined for a task list operation are recorded and compared to predefined specifications. The inspection results for a single inspection lot can be recorded using the Results Recording function. In turn, the inspection results for a number of inspection lots can be recorded using the Results Recording Worklist function.

Q-04:   A. Process a calibration inspection using a maintenance task list

A maintenance plan is the central planning object for a calibration inspection. The maintenance plan controls the type and scope of inspection activities to be performed, as well as if the activities will be performed on a performance or time-basis. As a maintenance plan is scheduled, maintenance calls are created and a maintenance order is generated. As the maintenance order is created and released, an inspection lot is created and the inspection lot quantity is determined based on the quantity of test equipment that is referenced in the maintenance order. Next, the task list is selected, the calibration inspection is conducted, the inspection results are recorded and the usage decision is documented. The completion of the inspection triggers an update to the equipment status in the equipment master record on the basis of the test equipment valuation documented by the usage decision that is recorded for the inspection lot.   In turn, the appraisal activities of the calibration inspection are confirmed for the maintenance order.

Q-05:   A. Select the "inspection points based on equipment" inspection point type in the task list header and C. Select the "inspection points based on the inspection lot quantity" control indicator in the sampling procedure assigned to the task list characteristic

Inspection points are used if a task list operation requires that multiple pieces of test equipment be inspected and characteristic results for each piece of equipment be recorded. Each inspection point relates to one piece of test equipment and is represented by a unique equipment number. During planning, inspection point data is maintained in the maintenance task list at the header and operation level and in the sampling procedure at the characteristic level. For example, the "inspection points based on equipment" inspection point type must be specified in the task list header and the manual or automatic test equipment valuation control indicator must be selected in the task list operation. In turn, the "inspection points based on inspection lot quantity" identifier must be specified in the sampling procedure that is defined for the inspection characteristic in the maintenance task list. This control indicator determines if inspection points are created for an inspection lot, and, if so, the inspection point type and the number of inspection points that should be created.

Q-06:   B. Create a defect record to document the critical damage to or defect in a piece of test equipment that is identified during the inspection

The results of a calibration inspection are recorded in the system as either characteristic values or defects. A defect record is created in the instance that a particular property of a piece of test equipment does not adhere to a specification that is defined for the inspection characteristic. When the defect record is initially stored in the system, it is assigned two statuses: outstanding quality notification and outstanding defect record. For critical defects, the outstanding notification can be automatically activated on the basis of a defect class. Following activation, the Notification functions are used to analyze the origin of a recorded defect and process resolutions to the defects that were originally documented in the defect records. The notification is completed when the documented issue is resolved. In turn, outstanding defect records that pertain to non-critical issues are not activated as a notification. Instead, these records are automatically completed when the usage decision for the inspection lot is entered to the system.

Q-07:   A. Create an inspection lot data record and document the required information in the record

A maintenance order is created when the proper function of a piece of test equipment must be confirmed. When the order is released, an inspection lot data record is generated. In the process, the inspection specifications for the test equipment are generated, the quantity of equipment to be inspected is confirmed, and inspection characteristics that must be inspected multiple times are identified. At the conclusion of the calibration inspection, results are recorded and the usage decision for the test equipment is documented in the data record using the functions of the Quality Management component.

Q-08:   B. Each characteristic of the test equipment and the test equipment itself is valuated on the basis of the recorded inspection results and valuation rules and C. The valuation of each characteristic and each piece of equipment is performed using a manual or automatic Results Recording function

A calibration inspection is conducted to determine the condition of a piece of test equipment. The inspection ensures that adverse factors that are discovered during an inspection, which affect the valuation of test equipment, are documented and drawn to the attention of management. During the inspection, inspection results are recorded as either characteristic values or defects. The equipment valuation that follows the inspection reflects a company's decision to accept or reject a piece of equipment for its intended purpose on the basis of the inspection results documented during the calibration inspection. The valuation of characteristics and the test equipment can be performed using a manual or automatic Results Recording function.

Q-09:   B. Use an automated procedure to activate an outstanding notification to efficiently address the defect or damage

The results of a calibration inspection are recorded in the system as either characteristic values or defects. A defect record is created in the instance that a particular property of a piece of test equipment does not adhere to a specification that is defined for the inspection characteristic. When the defect record is initially stored in the system, it is assigned two statuses: outstanding quality notification and outstanding defect record. For critical defects, the outstanding notification can be automatically activated on the basis of a defect class. Following activation, the Notification functions are used to analyze the origin of a recorded defect and process resolutions to the defects that were originally documented in the defect records. The notification is completed when the documented issue is resolved. In turn, outstanding defect records that pertain to non-critical issues are not activated as a notification. Instead, these records are automatically completed when the usage decision for the inspection lot is entered to the system.

Q-10:   B. Test Equipment Tracking Report

Some test equipment fails shortly after it has been inspected and found to meet the quality specifications defined for the equipment. As a result, a company requires the ability to identify quality inspections that were conducted with the equipment to determine if inspection results obtained with the equipment were valid or if issues with equipment led to erroneous test results. In the latter instance, the company must then determine if the inspections must be repeated. The Test Equipment Tracking Report accommodates this requirement by identifying the inspection characteristics that were evaluated with a particular piece of test equipment. In addition, the tracking report identifies the work center at which an inspection occurred and the time period during which the test equipment was located at the work center.

Q-11:   A. Activate an outstanding notification

The results of a calibration inspection are recorded in the system as either characteristic values or defects. A defect record is created in the instance that a particular property of a piece of test equipment does not adhere to a specification that is defined for the inspection characteristic. When the defect record is initially stored in the system, it is assigned two statuses: outstanding quality notification and outstanding defect record. For critical defects, the outstanding notification can be automatically activated on the basis of a defect class. Following activation, the Notification functions are used to analyze the origin of a recorded defect and process resolutions to the defects that were originally documented in the defect records. The notification is completed when the documented issue is resolved. In turn, outstanding defect records that pertain to non-

141

critical issues are not activated as a notification. Instead, these records are automatically completed when the usage decision for the inspection lot is entered to the system.

Q-12:   A. Sampling procedure

Samples are taken from a population to determine the characteristics of the population. The inspection of a piece of test equipment in the sample provides a means to verify whether or not the equipment conforms to particular technical specifications and if the test equipment is accepted or rejected for its intended purpose. During this process, one or more characteristics of the equipment may be inspected multiple times and, in turn, repeat measurements documented. These repeat measurements are triggered by the sampling procedure assigned to a characteristic, which determines both how the system calculates a sample size and the basis on which an inspection characteristic is valuated.

Q-13:   C. Create an inspection instruction and trigger its printout by means of the calculation of a sample size

An inspector receives information regarding the conduct of a calibration inspection by means of an inspection instruction. This instruction is derived from data in both the inspection plan and the inspection lot. Such data includes the description of the material to be inspected, the inspection date, the inspection lot number and the inspection operations and inspection characteristics. Also included are the inspection method and inspection specifications that are defined for each characteristic. The creation and printout of the instruction is triggered by the calculation of a sample size, the creation of the inspection lot or as determined by the user.

Q-14:   A. Update the equipment status in the equipment master record on the basis of the usage decision code that is entered for the inspection lot following a calibration inspection

The entry of a usage decision for an inspection lot concludes the calibration inspection. On the basis of the usage decision code, particular follow-up functions can be triggered. One such follow-up function is the calculation of a quality score for the inspection lot. Other follow-up actions include the update of the inspection interval in the preventive maintenance plan using the cycle modification factor and the creation of measurement documents in which to record the inspection results for measurement points. Also performed following the conclusion of a calibration inspection are the update of the status of PRT-relevant equipment in the equipment master record to reflect the valuation of the equipment and to control the release of the equipment for future use and the technical completion of a maintenance order, which denotes the completion of planned activities for the maintenance order.

Q-15:   A. Change the cycle modification factor in the maintenance plan as the usage decision is entered to shorten an inspection interval

143

A PM maintenance plan is the central planning object for a calibration inspection. The maintenance plan controls the type and scope of inspection activities to be performed and whether the activities are performed on a time or performance-basis. The cycle modification factor is an element of the maintenance plan that is used to alter a plan's time-based or performance-based maintenance cycle to best reflect the actual condition and maintenance requirements of a piece of test equipment. The inspection interval must be revised if the test equipment status, which is documented in the equipment master record, does not reflect the actual condition of the test equipment and if the equipment may require maintenance prior to the next scheduled inspection. In this instance, to preclude the possibility that the equipment may fail prior to the next subsequent inspection, the cycle modification factor in the maintenance plan is changed to reduce the inspection interval as the inspection lot usage decision is documented.

Q-16:   A. A usage list created with the Test Equipment Tracking function

Some test equipment fails shortly after it has been inspected and found to meet the quality specifications defined for the equipment. As a result, a company requires the ability to identify quality inspections that were conducted with the equipment to determine if inspection results obtained with the equipment were valid or if issues with equipment led to erroneous test results. In the latter instance, the company must then determine if the inspections must be repeated. The Test

Equipment Tracking Report accommodates this requirement by identifying the inspection characteristics that were evaluated with a particular piece of test equipment. In addition, the tracking report identifies the work center at which an inspection occurred and the time period during which the test equipment was located at the work center.

Q-17:   A. Maintenance order

A maintenance plan is the central planning object for a calibration inspection. The maintenance plan controls the type and scope of inspection activities to be performed, as well as if the activities will be performed on a performance or time-basis. As a maintenance plan is scheduled, maintenance calls are created and a maintenance order is generated. As the maintenance order is created and released, an inspection lot is created and the inspection lot quantity is determined based on the quantity of test equipment that is referenced in the maintenance order. Next, the task list is selected, the calibration inspection is conducted, the inspection results are recorded and the usage decision is documented. The completion of the inspection triggers an update to the equipment status in the equipment master record on the basis of the test equipment valuation documented by the usage decision that is recorded for the inspection lot.   In turn, the appraisal activities of the calibration inspection are confirmed for the maintenance order.

Q-18:   A. Maintenance order

A maintenance plan is the central planning object for a calibration inspection. The maintenance plan controls the type and scope of inspection activities to be performed, as well as if the activities will be performed on a performance or time-basis. As a maintenance plan is scheduled, maintenance calls are created and a maintenance order is generated. As the maintenance order is created and released, an inspection lot is created and the inspection lot quantity is determined based on the quantity of test equipment that is referenced in the maintenance order. Next, the task list is selected, the calibration inspection is conducted, the inspection results are recorded and the usage decision is documented. The completion of the inspection triggers an update to the equipment status in the equipment master record on the basis of the test equipment valuation documented by the usage decision that is recorded for the inspection lot. In turn, the appraisal activities of the calibration inspection are confirmed for the maintenance order.

Q-19:   A. Inspection instruction

An inspector receives information regarding the conduct of a calibration inspection by means of an inspection instruction. This instruction is derived from data in both the inspection plan and the inspection lot. Such data includes the description of the material to be inspected, the inspection date, the inspection lot number and the inspection operations and inspection characteristics. Also included are the inspection method and inspection specifications that are defined for each characteristic. The creation and printout of the instruction is triggered by the calculation of a sample size, the creation of the inspection lot or as determined by the user.

Q-20:   A. Inspection instruction

An inspector receives information regarding the conduct of a calibration inspection by means of an inspection instruction. This instruction is derived from data in both the inspection plan and the inspection lot. Such data includes the description of the material to be inspected, the inspection date, the inspection lot number and the inspection operations and inspection characteristics. Also included are the inspection method and inspection specifications that are defined for each characteristic. The creation and printout of the instruction is triggered by the calculation of a sample size, the creation of the inspection lot or as determined by the user.

Q-21:   A. Maintenance task list header, B. Maintenance task list operation and C. Sampling procedure

Inspection points are used if a task list operation requires the inspection of test equipment multiple times and that characteristic results for each inspection point be recorded. The inspection point relates to one piece of test equipment and is represented by a unique equipment number. During planning, inspection point data is maintained in the maintenance task list at the header and operation level and in the sampling procedure at the characteristic level. For example, the "inspection points based on equipment" inspection point type must be specified in the task list header and the manual or automatic test equipment valuation control indicator must be selected in the task list operation. In turn, the "inspection points based on inspection lot quantity" identifier must be specified in the sampling procedure that is defined for the inspection characteristic in the maintenance task list.

Q-22:   A. Notification item

The results of a calibration inspection are recorded in the system as either characteristic values or defects. A defect record is created in the instance that a particular property of a piece of test equipment does not adhere to a specification that is defined for the inspection characteristic. When the defect record is initially stored in the system, it is assigned two statuses: outstanding quality notification and outstanding defect record. For critical defects, the outstanding notification can be automatically activated on the basis of a defect class. Following activation, the Notification functions are used to analyze the origin of a recorded defect and process resolutions to the defects that were originally documented in the defect records. The notification is completed when the documented issue is resolved. In turn, outstanding defect records that pertain to non-critical issues are not activated as a notification. Instead, these records are automatically completed when the usage decision for the inspection lot is entered to the system.

Q-23:   B. Inspection type defined in the maintenance
plan

A maintenance plan is the central planning object for a
calibration inspection. The maintenance plan controls
the type and scope of inspection activities to be
performed, as well as if the activities will be performed
on a performance or time-basis. As a maintenance plan
is scheduled, maintenance calls are created and a
maintenance order is generated. As the maintenance
order is created and released, an inspection lot is
created and the inspection lot quantity is determined
based on the quantity of test equipment that is
referenced in the maintenance order. Next, the task list
is selected, the calibration inspection is conducted, the
inspection results are recorded and the usage decision is
documented. The completion of the inspection triggers
an update to the equipment status in the equipment
master record on the basis of the test equipment
valuation documented by the usage decision that is
recorded for the inspection lot.   In turn, the appraisal
activities of the calibration inspection are confirmed for
the maintenance order.

Q-24:   A. Results Recording

The results of a calibration inspection are recorded in
the system as either characteristic values or defects. A
defect record is created in the instance that a particular
property of a piece of test equipment does not adhere
to a specification that is defined for the inspection
characteristic. When the defect record is initially stored
in the system, it is assigned two statuses: outstanding

quality notification and outstanding defect record. For critical defects, the outstanding notification can be automatically activated on the basis of a defect class. Following activation, the Notification functions are used to analyze the origin of a recorded defect and process resolutions to the defects that were originally documented in the defect records. The notification is completed when the documented issue is resolved. In turn, outstanding defect records that pertain to non-critical issues are not activated as a notification. Instead, these records are automatically completed when the usage decision for the inspection lot is entered to the system.

Q-25:   A. Maintenance order and B. Inspection characteristic control key in inspection operation

Samples are taken from a population to determine the characteristics of Samples are taken from a population to determine the characteristics of the population. The inspection of a piece of test equipment in the sample provides a means to verify whether or not the equipment conforms to particular technical specifications and if the test equipment is accepted or rejected for its intended purpose. During this process, one or more characteristics of the equipment may be inspected multiple times and, in turn, repeat measurements documented. These repeat measurements are triggered by the sampling procedure, which determines both how the system calculates a sample size and the basis on which an inspection characteristic is valuated. Repeat measurements also require that the creation of the inspection lot be triggered by a maintenance order and the selection of an inspection characteristic control key for the inspection operation

Q-26:   A. Maintenance Notification

The results of a calibration inspection are recorded in the system as either characteristic values using the Results Recording function or defects using the Defects Recording function. A defect record is created in the instance that a particular property of a piece of test equipment does not adhere to a specification that is defined for the inspection characteristic. When the defect record is initially stored in the system, it is assigned two statuses: outstanding quality notification and outstanding defect record. For critical defects, the outstanding notification can be automatically activated on the basis of a defect class. Following activation, the Notification functions are used to analyze the origin of a recorded defect. The notification is completed when the documented issue is resolved. In turn, the outstanding defect records that pertain to non-critical issues are not activated as a notification but rather are automatically completed when the usage decision for the inspection lot is entered to the system.

Q-27:   C. Assignment of defect class to defect code

The results of a calibration inspection are recorded in the system as either characteristic values or defects. A defect record is created in the instance that a particular property of a piece of test equipment does not adhere to a specification that is defined for the inspection

characteristic. When the defect record is initially stored in the system, it is assigned two statuses: outstanding quality notification and outstanding defect record. For a critical defect, the outstanding notification can be automatically activated on the basis of a defect class that is assigned to a defect code. This activation requires the assignment of the maintenance notification type to the calibration inspection type, the selection of the defects recording control indicator for the inspection characteristics and the assignment of a defect class to a defect code. Following the activation of the notification, the Notifications functions support the analysis of the origin of the recorded defect and the processing of a resolution to the defect. The notification is completed when the documented issue is resolved. In turn, an outstanding defect record, that pertains to a non-critical issue, is not activated as a notification, but rather is automatically completed when the usage decision for the inspection lot is documented in the system.

Q-28:   A. Test Equipment Tracking Report

Some test equipment fails shortly after it has been inspected and found to meet the quality specifications defined for the equipment. As a result, a company requires the ability to identify quality inspections that were conducted with the equipment to determine if inspection results obtained with the equipment were valid or if issues with equipment led to erroneous test results. In the latter instance, the company must then determine if the inspections must be repeated. The Test Equipment Tracking Report accommodates this requirement by identifying the inspection characteristics that were evaluated with a particular piece of test equipment. In addition, the tracking report identifies the work center at which an inspection occurred and the time period during which the test equipment was located at the work center.

Q-29:   A. Inspection point

Inspection points are used if a task list operation requires that multiple pieces of test equipment be inspected and characteristic results for each piece of equipment be recorded. Each inspection point relates to one piece of test equipment and is represented by a unique equipment number. During planning, inspection point data is maintained in the maintenance task list at the header and operation level and in the sampling procedure at the characteristic level. For example, the "inspection points based on equipment" inspection point type must be specified in the task list header and the manual or automatic test equipment valuation control indicator must be selected in the task list operation. In turn, an "inspection points based on inspection lot quantity" identifier must be specified in the sampling procedure that is assigned to the inspection characteristic in the maintenance task list.

Q-30:   B. Maintenance order

A maintenance plan is the central planning object for a calibration inspection. The maintenance plan controls the type and scope of inspection activities to be performed, as well as if the activities will be performed on a performance or time-basis. As a maintenance plan is scheduled, maintenance calls are created and a maintenance order is generated. As the maintenance order is created and released, an inspection lot is created with which to manage the inspection specifications and the inspection results. The inspection lot quantity is determined based on the quantity of test equipment that is referenced in the maintenance order. Next, the task list is selected, the calibration inspection is conducted, the inspection results are recorded and the usage decision is documented. The completion of the inspection triggers an update to the equipment status in the equipment master record on the basis of the test equipment valuation documented by the usage decision that is recorded for the inspection lot. In turn, the appraisal activities of the calibration inspection are confirmed for the maintenance order.

Q-31:   A. Master inspection characteristics in maintenance task list and measuring point master records linked by class characteristics

A usage decision code is entered for an inspection lot at the conclusion of an inspection to document the suitability of test equipment for its intended purpose. The Test Equipment Management system automatically executes particular follow-up actions on the basis of a usage decision code. One such follow-up action is the creation of a measurement document for each inspection point that is defined for the test equipment. The results of the calibration inspection are recorded in measurement documents, which are stored in the test equipment history. The requirements of this function include the linkage of the master inspection characteristic in the maintenance task list and the measuring point master records by means of the class characteristics.

Q-32:   A. Maintenance notification

The results of a calibration inspection are recorded in the system as either characteristic values or defects. A defect record is created in the instance that a particular property of a piece of test equipment does not adhere to a specification that is defined for the inspection characteristic. When the defect record is initially stored in the system, it is assigned two statuses: outstanding quality notification and outstanding defect record. For a critical defect, the outstanding notification can be automatically activated on the basis of a defect class that is assigned to a defect code. Following the activation of the notification, the Notifications functions support the analysis of the origin of the recorded defect and the processing of a resolution to the defect. The notification is completed when the documented issue is resolved.

Q-33:   A. Usage Decision

The entry of a usage decision code for an inspection lot concludes the calibration inspection and documents the inspection's outcome. On the basis of the usage decision code, individual follow-up functions can be triggered. One such follow-up function is the calculation of a quality score for the inspection lot. A quality score is a statistical value that represents the quality of the material in the inspection lot. This quality score might be a specific value that's defined for the usage decision code determined by a share of the defects in an inspection lot, a share of the defects for a characteristic or the quality score for characteristics. The automatic calculation of a quality score requires that a quality score determination process be defined for a material master inspection type.

Q-34:   A. Usage Decision

The entry of a usage decision for an inspection lot concludes the calibration inspection. On the basis of the usage decision code, particular follow-up functions can be triggered. One such follow-up function is the calculation of a quality score for the inspection lot. Other follow-up actions include the update of the inspection interval in the preventive maintenance plan using the cycle modification factor and the creation of measurement documents in which to record the inspection results for measurement points. Also performed following the conclusion of a calibration inspection are the update of the status of PRT-relevant equipment in the equipment master record to reflect the valuation of the equipment and to control the release of the equipment for future use and the technical completion of a maintenance order, which denotes the completion of planned activities for the maintenance order.

Q-35:   A. Usage Decision

The entry of a usage decision for an inspection lot concludes the calibration inspection. On the basis of the usage decision code, particular follow-up functions can be triggered. One such follow-up function is the calculation of a quality score for the inspection lot. Other follow-up actions include the update of the inspection interval in the preventive maintenance plan using the cycle modification factor and the creation of measurement documents in which to record the inspection results for measurement points. Also performed following the conclusion of a calibration inspection are the update of the status of PRT-relevant equipment in the equipment master record to reflect the valuation of the equipment and to control the release of the equipment for future use and the technical completion of a maintenance order, which denotes the completion of planned activities for the maintenance order.

Q-36:   A. Usage decision code

A PM maintenance plan is the central planning object for a calibration inspection. The maintenance plan controls the type and scope of inspection activities to be performed and whether the activities are performed on a time or performance-basis. The cycle modification factor is an element of the maintenance plan that is used to alter a plan's time-based or performance-based maintenance cycle to best reflect the actual condition and maintenance requirements of a piece of test equipment. The inspection interval must be revised if the test equipment status, which is documented in the equipment master record, does not reflect the actual condition of the test equipment and if the equipment may require maintenance prior to the next scheduled inspection. In this instance, to preclude the possibility that the equipment may fail prior to the next subsequent inspection, the cycle modification factor in the maintenance plan is changed to reduce the inspection interval as the inspection lot usage decision is documented.

Q-37:   A. Usage Decision

The entry of a usage decision for an inspection lot concludes the calibration inspection. On the basis of the usage decision code, particular follow-up functions can be triggered. One such follow-up function is the calculation of a quality score for the inspection lot. Other follow-up actions include the update of the inspection interval in the preventive maintenance plan using the cycle modification factor and the creation of measurement documents in which to record the inspection results for measurement points. Also performed following the conclusion of a calibration inspection are the update of the status of PRT-relevant equipment in the equipment master record to reflect the valuation of the equipment and to control the release of the equipment for future use and the technical completion of a maintenance order, which denotes the completion of planned activities for the maintenance order.

Q-38:   A. Maintenance notification item is recorded at the time a critical defect is recorded

The results of a calibration inspection are recorded in the system as either characteristic values or defects. A defect record is created in the instance that a particular property of a piece of test equipment does not adhere to a specification that is defined for the inspection characteristic. When the defect record is initially stored in the system, it is assigned two statuses: outstanding quality notification and outstanding defect record. For a critical defect, the outstanding notification can be automatically activated on the basis of a defect class that is assigned to a defect code. Following the activation of the notification, the Notifications functions support the analysis of the origin of the recorded defect and the processing of a resolution to the defect. The notification is completed when the documented issue is resolved.

Q-39: A. The ability to create inspection instructions to describe the processes required to draw a sample and conduct an inspection at a particular work center and B. The ability to create an inspection instruction to define the inspection specification for each characteristic

An inspector receives information regarding the conduct of a calibration inspection by means of an inspection instruction. This instruction is derived from data in both the inspection plan and the inspection lot. Such data includes the description of the material to be inspected, the inspection date, the inspection lot number and the inspection characteristics. Also included are the inspection method, inspection specifications that are defined for each characteristic and descriptions of the processes required to draw a sample. The printout of the instruction is triggered by the calculation of a sample size, the creation of the inspection lot or as determined by the user.

Q-40: A. The ability to define the cycle modification factor for the maintenance plan and B. The ability to define preventive maintenance cycles in the maintenance plan

A PM maintenance plan is the central planning object for a calibration inspection. The maintenance plan controls the type and scope of inspection activities to be performed and whether the activities are performed on a time or performance-basis. The cycle modification factor is an element of the maintenance plan that is used to alter a plan's time-based or performance-based maintenance cycle to best reflect the actual condition and maintenance requirements of a piece of test equipment. The inspection interval must be revised if the test equipment status, which is documented in the equipment master record, does not reflect the actual condition of the test equipment and if the equipment may require maintenance prior to the next scheduled inspection. In this instance, to preclude the possibility that the equipment may fail prior to the next subsequent inspection, the cycle modification factor in the maintenance plan is changed to reduce the inspection interval as the inspection lot usage decision is documented.

Q-41: A. Assignment of sampling procedures to inspection characteristics in the master task list

Samples are taken from a population to determine the characteristics of the population. The inspection of a piece of test equipment in the sample provides a means to verify whether or not the equipment conforms to particular technical specifications and if the test equipment is accepted or rejected for its intended purpose. During this process, one or more characteristics of the equipment may be inspected multiple times and, in turn, repeat measurements documented. These repeat measurements are triggered by the sampling procedure, which determines both how the system calculates a sample size and the basis on which an inspection characteristic is valuated.

Q-42:   A. Predefined specifications for inspection characteristics are defined in the maintenance task list and B. Automatic valuation of test equipment using the valuation mode that is set for an inspection point in the material task list

A calibration inspection is conducted to determine the condition of a piece of test equipment. The inspection ensures that the equipment is in good condition or, if not, allows the company to make arrangements for its repair or replacement The equipment valuation that is documented at the conclusion of an inspection reflects a company's decision to accept or reject the equipment for its intended purpose on the basis of recorded inspection results. During the conduct of an inspection, predefined inspection specifications for inspection characteristics are defined in the maintenance task list and each characteristic of the test equipment is valuated, as is the test equipment itself on the basis of

161

recorded inspection results and valuation rules that are defined in the valuation mode that is set for the inspection point in the material task list. The valuation of the characteristics and each piece of equipment can be performed using either a manual or automatic results recording function. Discovery of adverse factors that affect the test equipment valuation are documented and drawn to the attention of management by means of defect records and notifications.

Q-43:   A. Automatic proposal of follow-up action per the usage decision code

The entry of a usage decision for an inspection lot concludes the calibration inspection. On the basis of the usage decision code, particular follow-up functions can be triggered. One such follow-up function is the calculation of a quality score for the inspection lot. Other follow-up actions include the update of the inspection interval in the preventive maintenance plan using the cycle modification factor and the creation of measurement documents in which to record the inspection results for measurement points. Also performed following the conclusion of a calibration inspection are the update of the status of PRT-relevant equipment in the equipment master record to reflect the valuation of the equipment and to control the release of the equipment for future use and the technical completion of a maintenance order, which denotes the completion of planned activities for the maintenance order.

Q-44:   A. Automatic creation of inspection lot and B. Automatic execution of follow-up actions

A calibration inspection is conducted to determine the condition of a piece of test equipment. The inspection ensures that the equipment is in good condition or, if not, allows the company to make arrangements for its repair or replacement   Discovery of adverse factors that affect the test equipment valuation are documented and drawn to the attention of management. An equipment valuation reflects a company's decision to accept or reject a piece of equipment for its intended purpose on the basis of inspection results that are documented during a calibration inspection. Each characteristic of the test equipment is first valuated and then the test equipment itself is valuated on the basis of recorded inspection results and valuation rules. The valuation of the characteristics and each piece of equipment can be performed using either a manual or automatic results recording function although the automatic function is more efficient. The calibration inspection component minimizes any issues with conducting the steps of the inspection and valuating equipment by the automatic creation of inspection lots and execution of follow-up actions.

Q-45:   A. Automatic creation of inspection lot for the maintenance order

A maintenance plan, which consists of one or more maintenance items, is the central planning object for a calibration inspection. The plan controls the maintenance and inspection tasks to be performed on

163

maintenance objects and to schedule the performance of the tasks using time- and/or performance-based maintenance cycles, or inspection intervals. For example, test equipment calibration can occur each year on a key date or following 100 operations. As a maintenance plan is scheduled, maintenance calls are created that are converted to orders when the calls are due. Depending on Customizing settings, the system can automatically create and release the order and create an inspection lot. The maintenance task list, which determines the maintenance activities to be performed, is then selected and assigned to the maintenance plan. The maintenance task list structure contains both operations and sub-operations that describe the work to be performed during a calibration inspection and master inspection characteristics, which describe what is to be inspected. The characteristics include the quantitative and qualitative inspection specifications, such as tolerances. Following the selection of the task list, the calibration inspection operations can be performed in chronological order. After the inspection is conducted and inspection results are recorded, a usage decision for the inspection lot is documented and the inspection lot is completed. The completion of the calibration inspection triggers an update to the status of the test equipment in the equipment master record according to the test equipment valuation as documented by the usage decision for the inspection lot. In turn, the activities of the calibration inspection are confirmed for the maintenance order using either the Results Recording or Inspection Lot Completion functions.

Q-46:   B. Inspection characteristics control indicator is not selected for the operation

A maintenance plan, which consists of one or more maintenance items, is the central planning object for a calibration inspection. The plan controls the maintenance and inspection tasks to be performed on maintenance objects and to schedule the performance of the tasks using time- and/or performance-based maintenance cycles, or inspection intervals. For example, test equipment calibration can occur each year on a key date or following 100 operations. As a maintenance plan is scheduled, maintenance calls are created that are converted to orders when the calls are due. Depending on Customizing settings, the system can automatically create and release the order and create an inspection lot. The maintenance task list, which determines the maintenance activities to be performed, is then selected and assigned to the maintenance plan. The maintenance task list structure contains both operations and sub-operations that describe the work to be performed during a calibration inspection and, if the characteristics control indicator is selected for operations, master inspection characteristics, which describe what is to be inspected. The characteristics include the quantitative and qualitative inspection specifications, such as tolerances. Following the selection of the task list, the calibration inspection operations can be performed in chronological order. After the inspection is conducted and inspection results are recorded, a usage decision for the inspection lot is documented and the inspection lot is completed. The completion of the calibration inspection triggers an

165

update to the status of the test equipment in the equipment master record according to the test equipment valuation as documented by the usage decision for the inspection lot. In turn, the activities of the calibration inspection are confirmed for the maintenance order using either the Results Recording or Inspection Lot Completion functions.

Q-47:   A. Usage decision follow-up action "change cycle modification factor" in the maintenance plan

A PM maintenance plan is the central planning object for a calibration inspection. The maintenance plan controls the type and scope of inspection activities to be performed and whether the activities are performed on a time or performance-basis. The cycle modification factor is an element of the maintenance plan that is used to alter a plan's time-based or performance-based maintenance cycle to best reflect the actual condition and maintenance requirements of a piece of test equipment. The inspection interval must be revised if the test equipment status, which is documented in the equipment master record, does not reflect the actual condition of the test equipment and if the equipment may require maintenance prior to the next scheduled inspection.   In this instance, to preclude the possibility that the equipment may fail prior to the next subsequent inspection, the cycle modification factor in the maintenance plan is changed to reduce the inspection interval as the inspection lot usage decision is documented.

Q-48:   A. Proposed equipment master record status update by means of the Usage Decision follow-up function

The entry of a usage decision for an inspection lot concludes the calibration inspection. On the basis of the usage decision code, particular follow-up functions can be triggered. One such follow-up function is the calculation of a quality score for the inspection lot. Other follow-up actions include the update of the inspection interval in the preventive maintenance plan using the cycle modification factor and the creation of measurement documents in which to record the inspection results for measurement points. Also performed following the conclusion of a calibration inspection are the update of the status of PRT-relevant equipment in the equipment master record to reflect the valuation of the equipment and to control the release of the equipment for future use and the technical completion of a maintenance order, which denotes the completion of planned activities for the maintenance order.

Q-49:   A. Cycle modification factor is defined in maintenance plan

A PM maintenance plan is the central planning object for a calibration inspection. The maintenance plan controls the type and scope of inspection activities to be performed and whether the activities are performed on a time or performance-basis. The cycle modification factor is an element of the maintenance plan that is used to alter a plan's time-based or performance-based maintenance cycle to best reflect the actual condition and maintenance requirements of a piece of test equipment. The inspection interval must be revised if the test equipment status, which is documented in the equipment master record, does not reflect the actual condition of the test equipment and if the equipment may require maintenance prior to the next scheduled inspection. In this instance, to preclude the possibility that the equipment may fail prior to the next subsequent inspection, the cycle modification factor in the maintenance plan is changed to reduce the inspection interval as the inspection lot usage decision is documented.

Q-50:   A. Completion of the maintenance order on the basis of the inspection lot usage decision code

The entry of a usage decision for an inspection lot concludes the calibration inspection. On the basis of the usage decision code, particular follow-up functions can be triggered. One such follow-up function is the calculation of a quality score for the inspection lot. Other follow-up actions include the update of the inspection interval in the preventive maintenance plan using the cycle modification factor and the creation of measurement documents in which to record the inspection results for measurement points. Also performed following the conclusion of a calibration inspection are the update of the status of PRT-relevant equipment in the equipment master record to reflect the valuation of the equipment and to control the release of the equipment for future use and the technical completion of a maintenance order, which denotes the completion of planned activities for the maintenance order.

Q-51:   A. Test Equipment Tracking function and B. Test Equipment Usage List

Some test equipment fails shortly after it has been inspected and found to meet the quality specifications defined for the equipment. As a result, a company requires the ability to identify quality inspections that were conducted with the equipment to determine if inspection results obtained with the equipment were valid or if issues with equipment led to erroneous test results. In the latter instance, the company must then determine if the inspections must be repeated. The Test Equipment Tracking Report accommodates this requirement by identifying the inspection characteristics that were evaluated with a particular piece of test equipment. In addition, the tracking report identifies the work center at which an inspection occurred and the time period during which the test equipment was located at the work center.

Q-52:   A. Inspection point type is not defined in the maintenance task list header and B. Inspection point valuation mode is not defined at the operation level

Inspection points are used if a task list operation requires that multiple pieces of test equipment be inspected and characteristic results for each piece of equipment be recorded. Each inspection point relates to one piece of test equipment and is represented by a unique equipment number. During planning, inspection point data is maintained in the maintenance

169

task list at the header and operation level and in the sampling procedure at the characteristic level. For example, the "inspection points based on equipment" inspection point type must be specified in the task list header and the manual or automatic test equipment valuation control indicator must be selected in the task list operation. In turn, the "inspection points based on inspection lot quantity" identifier must be specified in the sampling procedure that is defined for the inspection characteristic in the maintenance task list.

Q-53:   B. The sampling procedure that is assigned to a characteristic includes valuation mode that requires a manual entry

The results of a calibration inspection are recorded in the system as either characteristic values or defects. A defect record is created in the instance that a particular property of a piece of test equipment does not adhere to a specification that is defined for the inspection characteristic. When the defect record is initially stored in the system, it is assigned two statuses: outstanding quality notification and outstanding defect record. For critical defects, the outstanding notification can be automatically activated on the basis of a defect class. Following activation, the Notification functions are used to analyze the origin of a recorded defect and process resolutions to the defects that were originally documented in the defect records. The notification is completed when the documented issue is resolved. In turn, outstanding defect records that pertain to non-critical issues are not activated as a notification. Instead, these records are automatically completed when the

170

usage decision for the inspection lot is entered to the system. The activation of the notification requires the assignment of the maintenance notification type to the calibration inspection type, the selection of the defects recording control indicator for the inspection characteristics and the assignment of a defect class to a defect code.

Q-54:   A. The maintenance notification type is not assigned to the inspection type in Customizing and B. The defects recording control indicator for the inspection characteristic is not set

The results of a calibration inspection are recorded in the system as either characteristic values or defects. A defect record is created in the instance that a particular property of a piece of test equipment does not adhere to a specification that is defined for the inspection characteristic. When the defect record is initially stored in the system, it is assigned two statuses: outstanding quality notification and outstanding defect record. For a critical defect, the outstanding notification can be automatically activated on the basis of a defect class that is assigned to a defect code. This activation requires the assignment of the maintenance notification type to the calibration inspection type, the selection of the defects recording control indicator for the inspection characteristics and the assignment of a defect class to a defect code. Following the activation of the notification, the Notifications functions support the analysis of the origin of the recorded defect and the processing of a resolution to the defect. The notification is completed when the documented issue is resolved.

Q-55:   A. A piece of equipment has not yet been valuated for an inspection operation and B. The customer does not have the authorization to enter the usage decision for the inspection lot

A calibration inspection is conducted to determine the condition of a piece of test equipment. The inspection ensures that adverse factors that are discovered during an inspection, which affect the valuation of test equipment, are documented and drawn to the attention of management. During the inspection, inspection results are recorded as either characteristic values or defects. The equipment valuation that follows the inspection reflects a company's decision to accept or reject a piece of equipment for its intended purpose on the basis of the inspection results documented during the calibration inspection. This process requires that both the characteristics of the test equipment and the test equipment itself be valuated on the basis of the recorded inspection results and valuation rules. The valuation of characteristics and the test equipment can be performed using a manual or automatic Results Recording function by a user who is assigned the appropriate system authorization.

Q-56:   A. The equipment type of the test equipment is not PRT-relevant

The entry of a usage decision for an inspection lot concludes the calibration inspection. On the basis of the usage decision code, particular follow-up functions can be triggered. One such follow-up function is the calculation of a quality score for the inspection lot. Other follow-up actions include the update of the inspection interval in the preventive maintenance plan using the cycle modification factor and the creation of measurement documents in which to record the inspection results for measurement points. Also performed following the conclusion of a calibration inspection are the update of the status of PRT-relevant equipment in the equipment master record to reflect the valuation of the equipment and to control the release of the equipment for future use and the technical completion of a maintenance order, which denotes the completion of planned activities for the maintenance order.

Q-57:   A. The cycle modification factor was not adjusted subsequent to the calibration inspection to shorten the inspection interval

A PM maintenance plan is the central planning object for a calibration inspection. The maintenance plan controls the type and scope of inspection activities to be performed and whether the activities are performed on a time or performance-basis. The cycle modification factor is an element of the maintenance plan that is used to alter a plan's maintenance cycle to best reflect the actual condition and maintenance requirements of a piece of test equipment. The inspection interval must be revised if the test equipment status, which is documented in the equipment master record, does not reflect the actual condition of the test equipment and if the equipment may require maintenance prior to the next scheduled inspection. In this instance, to preclude the possibility that the equipment may fail prior to the next subsequent inspection, the cycle modification factor in the maintenance plan is changed to reduce the inspection interval as the inspection lot usage decision is documented.

Q-58: A. The master inspection characteristics assigned to the maintenance task list are not linked to the measuring point master records by means of class characteristics

A usage decision code is entered for an inspection lot at the conclusion of an inspection to document the suitability of test equipment for its intended purpose. The Test Equipment Management system automatically executes particular follow-up actions on the basis of a usage decision code. One such follow-up action is the creation of measurement document for each inspection point that is defined for the test equipment. The results of the calibration inspection are recorded in the measurement documents that are associated with measurement points, which are stored in the test equipment history. The requirements of this function include the linkage of the master inspection characteristic in the maintenance task list and the measuring point master records by means of the class characteristics.

Q-59: B. The equipment is not identified as a production resource/tool in the task list operation and

C. The test equipment is not assigned to the inspection characteristic

Some test equipment fails shortly after it has been inspected and found to meet the quality specifications defined for the equipment. As a result, a company requires the ability to identify quality inspections that were conducted with the equipment to determine if inspection results obtained with the equipment were valid or if issues with equipment led to erroneous test results. In the latter instance, the company must then determine if the inspections must be repeated. The Test Equipment Tracking Report accommodates this requirement by identifying the inspection characteristics that were evaluated with a particular piece of test equipment. In addition, the tracking report identifies the work center at which an inspection occurred and the time period during which the test equipment was located at the work center. The creation of the Test Equipment Tracking Report requires the creation of an equipment master record for the test equipment, a reference to the equipment as a production resource tool in the task list operation, the assignment of the test equipment to a characteristic in the task list and the identification of a work center in the task list operation.

Q-60:   B. Inspection type is not assigned to notification type

The results of a calibration inspection are recorded in the system as either characteristic values or defects. A defect record is created in the instance that a particular property of a piece of test equipment does not adhere to a specification that is defined for the inspection

characteristic. When the defect record is initially stored in the system, it is assigned two statuses: outstanding quality notification and outstanding defect record. For critical defects, the outstanding notification can be automatically activated on the basis of a defect class. Following activation, the Notification functions are used to analyze the origin of a recorded defect and process resolutions to the defects that were originally documented in the defect records. The notification is completed when the documented issue is resolved. In turn, outstanding defect records that pertain to non-critical issues are not activated as a notification. Instead, these records are automatically completed when the usage decision for the inspection lot is entered to the system. The activation of the notification requires the assignment of the maintenance notification type to the calibration inspection type, the selection of the defects recording control indicator for the inspection characteristics and the assignment of a defect class to a defect code.

Q-61:   A. Measuring point master records and master inspection characteristics must be linked by means of class characteristics to create measurement documents

A usage decision code is entered for an inspection lot at the conclusion of an inspection to document the suitability of test equipment for its intended purpose. The Test Equipment Management system automatically executes particular follow-up actions on the basis of a usage decision code. One such follow-up action is the creation of measurement document for each inspection point that is defined for the test equipment. The results of the calibration inspection are recorded in the measurement documents, which are stored in the test equipment history. The requirements of this function include the linkage of the master inspection characteristic in the maintenance task list and the measuring point master records by means of the class characteristics.

Q-62:   C. Maintenance notification type is assigned to the calibration inspection type in Customizing

The results of a calibration inspection are recorded in the system as either characteristic values or defects. A defect record is created in the instance that a particular property of a piece of test equipment does not adhere to a specification that is defined for the inspection characteristic. When the defect record is initially stored in the system, it is assigned two statuses: outstanding quality notification and outstanding defect record. For critical defects, the outstanding notification can be automatically activated on the basis of a defect class. Following activation, the Notification functions are used to analyze the origin of a recorded defect and process resolutions to the defects that were originally documented in the defect records. The notification is completed when the documented issue is resolved. In turn, outstanding defect records that pertain to non-critical issues are not activated as a notification. Instead, these records are automatically completed when the usage decision for the inspection lot is entered to the system. The activation of the notification requires the assignment of the maintenance notification type to the calibration inspection type, the selection of the defects recording control indicator for the inspection characteristics and the assignment of a defect class to a defect code.

Q-63:   B. Assignment of maintenance notification type to the calibration inspection type in the IMG

The results of a calibration inspection are recorded in the system as either characteristic values or defects. A defect record is created in the instance that a particular property of a piece of test equipment does not adhere to a specification that is defined for the inspection characteristic. When the defect record is initially stored in the system, it is assigned two statuses: outstanding quality notification and outstanding defect record. For critical defects, the outstanding notification can be automatically activated on the basis of a defect class. Following activation, the Notification functions are used to analyze the origin of a recorded defect and process resolutions to the defects that were originally documented in the defect records. The notification is completed when the documented issue is resolved. In turn, outstanding defect records that pertain to non-critical issues are not activated as a notification. Instead, these records are automatically completed when the usage decision for the inspection lot is entered to the system. The activation of the notification requires the assignment of the maintenance notification type to the calibration inspection type, the selection of the defects recording control indicator for the inspection characteristics and the assignment of a defect class to a defect code.

Q-64:   C. Sampling procedure

An inspection is conducted to determine if a material fulfills required quality criteria. To conduct the inspection, physical samples of the material or batch are selected and evaluated according to an inspection plan. Instructions for drawing the sample, such as the size of each physical sample and the number of samples to be taken are documented in a sample-drawing procedure, which is assigned to the inspection plan. The sampling type, which is defined in the sampling procedure, specifies how a sample is to be calculated. For example, 100 percent inspection, fixed sample or a sampling scheme. The sampling procedure also determines the criteria for lot acceptance by means of the valuation mode. Examples of valuation mode include attributive inspection per nonconforming units, variable inspection per s-method and no valuation parameters.

Q-65:   B. Sampling procedure

Samples are taken from a population to determine the characteristics of the population. The inspection of a piece of test equipment in the sample provides a means to verify whether or not the equipment conforms to particular technical specifications and if the test equipment is accepted or rejected for its intended purpose. During this process, one or more characteristics of the equipment may be inspected multiple times and, in turn, repeat measurements documented. These repeat measurements are triggered by the sampling procedure that's assigned to an inspection characteristic, which determines both how the system calculates a sample size and the basis on which an inspection characteristic is valuated.

Q-66:   A. Entry of equipment inspection point type in the maintenance task list header and C. Entry of the sampling procedure at the characteristic level of the maintenance task list

Inspection points are used if a task list operation requires that multiple pieces of test equipment be inspected and characteristic results for each piece of equipment be recorded. Each inspection point relates to one piece of test equipment and is represented by a unique equipment number. During planning, inspection point data is maintained in the maintenance task list at the header and operation level and in the sampling procedure at the characteristic level. For example, the "inspection points based on equipment" inspection point type must be specified in the task list header and the manual or automatic test equipment valuation control indicator must be selected in the task list operation. In turn, the "inspection points based on inspection lot quantity" identifier must be specified in the sampling procedure that is defined for the inspection characteristic in the maintenance task list.

Q-67:   B. Update the inspection interval in the preventive maintenance plan and C. Create measurement documents to record the inspection results for inspection points

The entry of a usage decision for an inspection lot concludes the calibration inspection. On the basis of the usage decision code, particular follow-up functions can be triggered. One such follow-up function is the calculation of a quality score for the inspection lot. Other follow-up actions include the update of the inspection interval in the preventive maintenance plan using the cycle modification factor and the creation of measurement documents in which to record the inspection results for measurement points. Also performed following the conclusion of a calibration inspection are the update of the status of PRT-relevant equipment in the equipment master record to reflect the valuation of the equipment and to control the release of the equipment for future use and the technical completion of a maintenance order, which denotes the completion of planned activities for the maintenance order.

Q-68:   A. Control the release of test equipment for future use on the basis of the results of previous calibration inspection

The entry of a usage decision for an inspection lot concludes the calibration inspection. On the basis of the usage decision code, particular follow-up functions can be triggered. One such follow-up function is the calculation of a quality score for the inspection lot. Other follow-up actions include the update of the inspection interval in the preventive maintenance plan using the cycle modification factor and the creation of measurement documents in which to record the inspection results for measurement points. Also

performed following the conclusion of a calibration inspection are the update of the status of PRT-relevant equipment in the equipment master record to reflect the valuation of the equipment and to control the release of the equipment for future use and the technical completion of a maintenance order, which denotes the completion of planned activities for the maintenance order.

Q-69:   A. Control the time period between one calibration inspection and the next

A PM maintenance plan is the central planning object for a calibration inspection. The maintenance plan controls the type and scope of inspection activities to be performed and whether the activities are performed on a time or performance-basis. The cycle modification factor is an element of the maintenance plan that is used to alter a plan's time-based or performance-based maintenance cycle to best reflect the actual condition and maintenance requirements of a piece of test equipment. The inspection interval must be revised if the test equipment status, which is documented in the equipment master record, does not reflect the actual condition of the test equipment and if the equipment may require maintenance prior to the next scheduled inspection. In this instance, to preclude the possibility that the equipment may fail prior to the next subsequent inspection, the cycle modification factor in the maintenance plan is changed to reduce the inspection interval as the inspection lot usage decision is documented.

Q-70:   C. Document the results of a calibration inspection for an inspection point

A usage decision code is entered for an inspection lot at the conclusion of an inspection to document the suitability of test equipment for its intended purpose. The Test Equipment Management system automatically executes particular follow-up actions on the basis of a usage decision code. One such follow-up action is the creation of measurement document for each inspection point that is defined for the test equipment. The results of the calibration inspection are recorded in measurement documents, which are stored in the test equipment history. The requirements of this function include the linkage of the master inspection characteristic in the maintenance task list and the measuring point master records by means of the class characteristics.

Q-71:   C. Denotes the completion of the planned activities for a maintenance order

The entry of a usage decision for an inspection lot concludes the calibration inspection. On the basis of the usage decision code, particular follow-up functions can be triggered. One such follow-up function is the calculation of a quality score for the inspection lot. Other follow-up actions include the update of the inspection interval in the preventive maintenance plan using the cycle modification factor and the creation of measurement documents in which to record the inspection results for measurement points. Also performed following the conclusion of a calibration

183

inspection are the update of the status of PRT-relevant equipment in the equipment master record to reflect the valuation of the equipment and to control the release of the equipment for future use and the technical completion of a maintenance order, which denotes the completion of planned activities for the maintenance order.

Q-72: B. Identify inspection characteristics that were inspected using a particular piece of test equipment

Some test equipment fails shortly after it has been inspected and found to meet the quality specifications defined for the equipment. As a result, a company requires the ability to identify quality inspections that were conducted with the equipment to determine if inspection results obtained with the equipment were valid or if issues with equipment led to erroneous test results. In the latter instance, the company must then determine if the inspections must be repeated. The Test Equipment Tracking Report accommodates this requirement by identifying the inspection characteristics that were evaluated with a particular piece of test equipment. In addition, the tracking report identifies the work center at which an inspection occurred and the time period during which the test equipment was located at the work center.

Q-73: A. Results Recording Worklist

After the inspection of a piece of test equipment, the inspection results for the individual characteristics that are defined for a task list operation are recorded and compared to predefined specifications. The inspection results for a single inspection lot can be recorded using the Results Recording function. In turn, the inspection results for a number of inspection lots can be recorded using the Results Recording Worklist function.

Q-74:   A. Results Recording Worklist, B. Manual Results Recording and C. Usage Decision

A calibration inspection is conducted to determine the condition of a piece of test equipment. The inspection ensures that adverse factors that are discovered during an inspection which affect the valuation of test equipment are documented and drawn to the attention of management. During the inspection, inspection results are recorded as either characteristic values or defects. The equipment valuation that follows the inspection reflects a company's decision to accept or reject a piece of equipment for its intended purpose on the basis of the recorded inspection results. This process requires that both the characteristics of the test equipment and the test equipment itself be valuated on the basis of the recorded inspection results and valuation rules. The valuation of characteristics and the test equipment can be performed using a manual or automatic Results Recording function.

Q-75:   A. Results Recording

After the inspection of a piece of test equipment, the inspection results for the individual characteristics that are defined for a task list operation are recorded and compared to predefined specifications. The inspection results for a single inspection lot can be recorded using the Results Recording function. In turn, the inspection results for a number of inspection lots can be recorded using the Results Recording Worklist function.

Q-76:   A. Usage Decision

The entry of a usage decision for an inspection lot concludes the calibration inspection. On the basis of the usage decision code, particular follow-up functions can be triggered. One such follow-up function is the calculation of a quality score for the inspection lot. Other follow-up actions include the update of the inspection interval in the preventive maintenance plan using the cycle modification factor and the creation of measurement documents in which to record the inspection results for measurement points. Also performed following the conclusion of a calibration inspection are the update of the status of PRT-relevant equipment in the equipment master record to reflect the valuation of the equipment and to control the release of the equipment for future use and the technical completion of a maintenance order, which denotes the completion of planned activities for the maintenance order.

Q-77:   A. Usage Decision

The entry of a usage decision for an inspection lot concludes the calibration inspection. On the basis of the usage decision code, particular follow-up functions can be triggered. One such follow-up function is the calculation of a quality score for the inspection lot. Other follow-up actions include the update of the inspection interval in the preventive maintenance plan using the cycle modification factor and the creation of measurement documents in which to record the inspection results for measurement points. Also performed following the conclusion of a calibration inspection are the update of the status of PRT-relevant equipment in the equipment master record to reflect the valuation of the equipment and to control the release of the equipment for future use and the technical completion of a maintenance order, which denotes the completion of planned activities for the maintenance order.

Q-78:   A. Usage Decision

The entry of a usage decision for an inspection lot concludes the calibration inspection. On the basis of the usage decision code, particular follow-up functions can be triggered. One such follow-up function is the calculation of a quality score for the inspection lot. Other follow-up actions include the update of the inspection interval in the preventive maintenance plan using the cycle modification factor and the creation of measurement documents in which to record the inspection results for measurement points. Also performed following the conclusion of a calibration inspection are the update of the status of PRT-relevant equipment in the equipment master record to reflect the valuation of the equipment and to control the release of the equipment for future use and the technical completion of a maintenance order, which denotes the completion of planned activities for the maintenance order.

187

Q-79:   A. Usage Decision

The entry of a usage decision for an inspection lot
concludes the calibration inspection. On the basis of
the usage decision code, particular follow-up functions
can be triggered. One such follow-up function is the
calculation of a quality score for the inspection lot.
Other follow-up actions include the update of the
inspection interval in the preventive maintenance plan
using the cycle modification factor and the creation of
measurement documents in which to record the
inspection results for measurement points. Also
performed following the conclusion of a calibration
inspection are the update of the status of PRT-relevant
equipment in the equipment master record to reflect
the valuation of the equipment and to control the
release of the equipment for future use and the
technical completion of a maintenance order, which
denotes the completion of planned activities for the
maintenance order.

Q-80:   A. Usage Decision

The entry of a usage decision for an inspection lot
concludes the calibration inspection. On the basis of
the usage decision code, particular follow-up functions
can be triggered. One such follow-up function is the
calculation of a quality score for the inspection lot.
Other follow-up actions include the update of the
inspection interval in the preventive maintenance plan
using the cycle modification factor and the creation of
measurement documents in which to record the
inspection results for measurement points. Also

performed following the conclusion of a calibration inspection are the update of the status of PRT-relevant equipment in the equipment master record to reflect the valuation of the equipment and to control the release of the equipment for future use and the technical completion of a maintenance order, which denotes the completion of planned activities for the maintenance order.

Q-81:   A. Test Equipment Tracking

Some test equipment fails shortly after it has been inspected and found to meet the quality specifications defined for the equipment. As a result, a company requires the ability to identify quality inspections that were conducted with the equipment to determine if inspection results obtained with the equipment were valid or if issues with equipment led to erroneous test results. In the latter instance, the company must then determine if the inspections must be repeated. The Test Equipment Tracking Report accommodates this requirement by identifying the inspection characteristics that were evaluated with a particular piece of test equipment. In addition, the tracking report identifies the work center at which an inspection occurred and the time period during which the test equipment was located at the work center.

Q-82:   A. A need exists to determine if a piece of equipment that is specified in a maintenance order meets a set of performance specifications and C. A need exists to determine if a piece of equipment that is specified in an inspection lot meets a set of performance specifications

The automatic or manual scheduling of a maintenance plan leads to the creation of a maintenance order. In turn, the release of the maintenance order leads to the creation of the inspection lot and the selection of the maintenance task list to be used for a calibration inspection. A calibration inspection of the test equipment is then conducted to verify that the test equipment that is specified in a maintenance order meets its predefined performance specifications.

Q-83:   A. Plant Maintenance

The functional integration of a business is mirrored in the integration of the Test Equipment Management functions with those of the Quality Management and Plant Maintenance components, each of which support the conduct of calibration inspections. Such components include the PM Technical Objects, PM Preventive Maintenance and PM Maintenance Processing components, the QM Quality Planning and QM Test Equipment Management components and the Classification System component.

Q-84:   B. Maintenance notification

The results of a calibration inspection are recorded in the system as either characteristic values or defects. A defect record is created in the instance that a particular property of a piece of test equipment does not adhere to a specification that is defined for the inspection

characteristic. When the defect record is initially stored in the system, it is assigned two statuses: outstanding quality notification and outstanding defect record. For critical defects, the outstanding notification can be automatically activated on the basis of a defect class. Following activation, the Notification functions are used to analyze the origin of a recorded defect and process resolutions to the defects that were originally documented in the defect records. The notification is completed when the documented issue is resolved. In turn, outstanding defect records that pertain to non-critical issues are not activated as a notification. Instead, these records are automatically completed when the usage decision for the inspection lot is entered to the system. The activation of the notification requires the assignment of the maintenance notification type to the calibration inspection type, the selection of the defects recording control indicator for the inspection characteristics and the assignment of a defect class to a defect code.

Q-85:   A. Document the existence of critical equipment defects that require analysis to determine a corrective action

The results of a calibration inspection are recorded in the system as either characteristic values or defects. A defect record is created in the instance that a particular property of a piece of test equipment does not adhere to a specification that is defined for the inspection characteristic. When the defect record is initially stored in the system, it is assigned two statuses: outstanding quality notification and outstanding defect record. For

191

critical defects, the outstanding notification can be automatically activated on the basis of a defect class. Following activation, the Notification functions are used to analyze the origin of a recorded defect and process resolutions to the defects that were originally documented in the defect records. The notification is completed when the documented issue is resolved. In turn, outstanding defect records that pertain to non-critical issues are not activated as a notification. Instead, these records are automatically completed when the usage decision for the inspection lot is entered to the system. The activation of the notification requires the assignment of the maintenance notification type to the calibration inspection type, the selection of the defects recording control indicator for the inspection characteristics and the assignment of a defect class to a defect code.

Q-86:   B. Requirement to shorten the equipment inspection interval and C. Requirement to create measurement documents for each measurement point

The entry of a usage decision for an inspection lot concludes the calibration inspection. On the basis of the usage decision code, particular follow-up functions can be triggered. One such follow-up function is the calculation of a quality score for the inspection lot. Other follow-up actions include the update of the inspection interval in the preventive maintenance plan using the cycle modification factor and the creation of measurement documents in which to record the inspection results for measurement points. Also performed following the conclusion of a calibration

inspection are the update of the status of PRT-relevant equipment in the equipment master record to reflect the valuation of the equipment and to control the release of the equipment for future use and the technical completion of a maintenance order, which denotes the completion of planned activities for the maintenance order.

Q-87:   Maintenance order

A maintenance order is created when the proper function of a piece of test equipment must be confirmed. When the order is released, an inspection lot data record is generated. In the process, the inspection specifications for the test equipment are generated, the quantity of equipment to be inspected is confirmed, and inspection characteristics that must be inspected multiple times are identified.

Q-88:   C. Inspection instruction

An inspector receives information regarding the conduct of a calibration inspection by means of an inspection instruction. This instruction is derived from data in both the inspection plan and the inspection lot. Such data includes the description of the material to be inspected, the inspection date, the inspection lot number and the inspection operations and inspection characteristics. Also included are the inspection method and inspection specifications that are defined for each characteristic. The creation and printout of the instruction is triggered by the calculation of a sample size, the creation of the inspection lot or as determined by the user.

Q-89:   A. True

Inspection points are used if a task list operation requires that multiple pieces of test equipment be inspected and characteristic results for each piece of equipment be recorded. Each inspection point relates to one piece of test equipment and is represented by a unique equipment number. During planning, inspection point data is maintained in the maintenance task list at the header and operation level and in the sampling procedure at the characteristic level. For example, the "inspection points based on equipment" inspection point type must be specified in the task list header and the manual or automatic test equipment valuation control indicator must be selected in the task list operation. In turn, the "inspection points based on inspection lot quantity" identifier must be specified in the sampling procedure that is defined for the inspection characteristic in the maintenance task list.

Q-90:   A. True

The results of a calibration inspection are recorded in the system as either characteristic values or defects. A defect record is created in the instance that a particular property of a piece of test equipment does not adhere to a specification that is defined for the inspection characteristic. The creation of the defect record does not require the documentation of the related characteristic in an inspection plan.

Q-91:   Notifications

The results of a calibration inspection are recorded in the system as either characteristic values or defects. A defect record is created in the instance that a particular property of a piece of test equipment does not adhere to a specification that is defined for the inspection characteristic. When the defect record is initially stored in the system, it is assigned two statuses: outstanding quality notification and outstanding defect record. For critical defects, the outstanding notification can be automatically activated on the basis of a defect class. Following activation, the Notification functions are used to analyze the origin of a recorded defect and process resolutions to the defects that were originally documented in the defect records. The notification is completed when the documented issue is resolved. In turn, outstanding defect records that pertain to non-critical issues are not activated as a notification. Instead, these records are automatically completed when the usage decision for the inspection lot is entered to the system. The activation of the notification requires the assignment of the maintenance notification type to the calibration inspection type, the selection of the defects recording control indicator for the inspection characteristics and the assignment of a defect class to a defect code.

Q-92:   A. True

Samples are taken from a population to determine the characteristics of the population. The inspection of a piece of test equipment in the sample provides a means to verify whether or not the equipment conforms to particular technical specifications and if the test equipment is accepted or rejected for its intended purpose. During this process, one or more characteristics of the equipment may be inspected multiple times and, in turn, repeat measurements documented. These repeat measurements are triggered by the sampling procedure, which determines both how the system calculates a sample size and the basis on which an inspection characteristic is valuated.

Q-93:   A. True

The entry of a usage decision code for an inspection lot concludes the calibration inspection and documents the inspection's outcome. On the basis of the usage decision code, individual follow-up functions can be triggered. One such follow-up function is the calculation of a quality score for the inspection lot. A quality score is a statistical value that represents the quality of the material in the inspection lot. This quality score might be a specific value that's defined for the usage decision code or a calculated value based on the share of defects in an inspection lot, the share of the defects for characteristic or the quality score for characteristics. The automatic calculation of a quality score requires that a quality score determination process be defined for a material master inspection type.

Q-94:   A. True

The entry of a usage decision for an inspection lot concludes the calibration inspection. On the basis of the usage decision code, particular follow-up functions can be triggered. One such follow-up function is the calculation of a quality score for the inspection lot. Other follow-up actions include the update of the inspection interval in the preventive maintenance plan using the cycle modification factor and the creation of measurement documents in which to record the inspection results for measurement points. Also performed following the conclusion of a calibration inspection are the update of the status of PRT-relevant equipment in the equipment master record to reflect the valuation of the equipment and to control the release of the equipment for future use and the technical completion of a maintenance order, which denotes the completion of planned activities for the maintenance order.

Q-95: B. Maintenance order

A maintenance order is created when the proper function of a piece of test equipment must be confirmed. When the order is released, an inspection lot data record is generated. In the process, the inspection specifications for the test equipment are generated, the quantity of equipment to be inspected is confirmed, and inspection characteristics that must be inspected multiple times are identified. At the conclusion of the calibration inspection, results are recorded and the usage decision for the test equipment is documented in the data record using the functions of the Quality Management component.

Q-96: A. True

The entry of a usage decision for an inspection lot concludes the calibration inspection. On the basis of the usage decision code, particular follow-up functions can be triggered. One such follow-up function is the calculation of a quality score for the inspection lot. Other follow-up actions include the update of the inspection interval in the preventive maintenance plan using the cycle modification factor and the creation of measurement documents in which to record the inspection results for measurement points. Also performed following the conclusion of a calibration inspection are the update of the status of PRT-relevant equipment in the equipment master record to reflect the valuation of the equipment and to control the release of the equipment for future use and the technical completion of a maintenance order, which denotes the completion of planned activities for the maintenance order.

Q-97:   B. Calculation of sample size

An inspector receives information regarding the conduct of a calibration inspection by means of an inspection instruction. This instruction is derived from data in both the inspection plan and the inspection lot. Such data includes the description of the material to be inspected, the inspection date, the inspection lot number and the inspection operations and inspection characteristics. Also included are the inspection method and inspection specifications that are defined for each characteristic. The printout of the instruction is triggered by the calculation of a sample size, the creation of the inspection lot or as determined by the user.

Q-98:   A. Characteristic specification and B. Inspection date

An inspector receives information regarding the conduct of a calibration inspection by means of an inspection instruction. This instruction is derived from data in both the inspection plan and the inspection lot. Such data includes the description of the material to be inspected, the inspection date, the inspection lot number and the inspection operations and inspection characteristics. Also included are the inspection method and inspection specifications that are defined for each characteristic. The printout of the instruction is triggered by the calculation of a sample size, the creation of the inspection lot or as determined by the user.

Q-99:   A. Sampling procedure and B. Maintenance task list

Inspection points are used if a task list operation requires that multiple pieces of test equipment be inspected and characteristic results for each piece of equipment be recorded. Each inspection point relates to one piece of test equipment and is represented by a unique equipment number. During planning, inspection point data is maintained in the maintenance task list at the header and operation level and in the sampling procedure at the characteristic level. For example, the "inspection points based on equipment"

199

inspection point type must be specified in the task list header and the manual or automatic test equipment valuation control indicator must be selected in the task list operation. In turn, the "inspection points based on inspection lot quantity" identifier must be specified in the sampling procedure that is defined for the inspection characteristic in the maintenance task list.

Q-100:   A. Assignment of maintenance notification type to the calibration inspection type in the task list header and B. Selection of defects recording control indicator in the inspection characteristic

The results of a calibration inspection are recorded in the system as either characteristic values or defects. A defect record is created in the instance that a particular property of a piece of test equipment does not adhere to a specification that is defined for the inspection characteristic. When the defect record is initially stored in the system, it is assigned two statuses: outstanding quality notification and outstanding defect record. For critical defects, the outstanding notification can be automatically activated on the basis of a defect class. Following activation, the Notification functions are used to analyze the origin of a recorded defect and process resolutions to the defects that were originally documented in the defect records. The notification is completed when the documented issue is resolved. In turn, outstanding defect records that pertain to non-critical issues are not activated as a notification. Instead, these records are automatically completed when the usage decision for the inspection lot is entered to the system. The activation of the notification requires the assignment of the maintenance notification type to the calibration inspection type, the selection of the defects recording control indicator for the inspection characteristics and the assignment of a defect class to a defect code.

Q-101:   A. The inspection point type is maintained in the maintenance task list header and C. The QM control indicator for inspection points based on the lot quantity is maintained in the sampling procedure

Inspection points are used if a task list operation requires that multiple pieces of test equipment be inspected and characteristic results for each piece of equipment be recorded. Each inspection point relates to one piece of test equipment and is represented by a unique equipment number. During planning, inspection point data is maintained in the maintenance task list at the header and operation level and in the sampling procedure at the characteristic level. For example, the "inspection points based on equipment" inspection point type must be specified in the task list header and the manual or automatic test equipment valuation control indicator must be selected in the task list operation. In turn, the "inspection points based on inspection lot quantity" identifier must be specified in the sampling procedure that is defined for the inspection characteristic in the maintenance task list.

Q-102:   A. Sampling procedure assigned to characteristics in a maintenance task list

Samples are taken from a population to determine the characteristics of the population. The inspection of a piece of test equipment in the sample provides a means to verify whether or not the equipment conforms to particular technical specifications and if the test equipment is accepted or rejected for its intended purpose. During this process, one or more characteristics of the equipment may be inspected multiple times and, in turn, repeat measurements documented. These repeat measurements are triggered by the sampling procedure that's assigned to an inspection characteristic, which determines both how the system calculates a sample size and the basis on which an inspection characteristic is valuated.

Q-103: A. Inspection type and B. Inspection characteristic

The results of a calibration inspection are recorded in the system as either characteristic values or defects. A defect record is created in the instance that a particular property of a piece of test equipment does not adhere to a specification that is defined for the inspection characteristic. When the defect record is initially stored in the system, it is assigned two statuses: outstanding quality notification and outstanding defect record. For critical defects, the outstanding notification can be automatically activated on the basis of a defect class. Following activation, the Notification functions are used to analyze the origin of a recorded defect and process resolutions to the defects that were originally documented in the defect records. The notification is completed when the documented issue is resolved. In

202

turn, outstanding defect records that pertain to non-critical issues are not activated as a notification. Instead, these records are automatically completed when the usage decision for the inspection lot is entered to the system. The activation of the notification requires the assignment of the maintenance notification type to the calibration inspection type, the selection of the defects recording control indicator for the inspection characteristics and the assignment of a defect class to a defect code.

Q-104:   B. Equipment master record

The entry of a usage decision for an inspection lot concludes the calibration inspection. On the basis of the usage decision code, particular follow-up functions can be triggered. One such follow-up function is the calculation of a quality score for the inspection lot. Other follow-up actions include the update of the inspection interval in the preventive maintenance plan using the cycle modification factor and the creation of measurement documents in which to record the inspection results for measurement points. Also performed following the conclusion of a calibration inspection are the update of the status of PRT-relevant equipment in the equipment master record to reflect the valuation of the equipment and to control the release of the equipment for future use and the technical completion of a maintenance order, which denotes the completion of planned activities for the maintenance order.

Q-105:   C. Maintenance plan

A PM maintenance plan is the central planning object for a calibration inspection. The maintenance plan controls the type and scope of inspection activities to be performed and whether the activities are performed on a time or performance-basis. The cycle modification factor is an element of the maintenance plan that is used to alter a plan's time-based or performance-based maintenance cycle to best reflect the actual condition and maintenance requirements of a piece of test equipment. The inspection interval must be revised if the test equipment status, which is documented in the equipment master record, does not reflect the actual condition of the test equipment and if the equipment may require maintenance prior to the next scheduled inspection. In this instance, to preclude the possibility that the equipment may fail prior to the next subsequent inspection, the cycle modification factor in the maintenance plan is changed to reduce the inspection interval as the inspection lot usage decision is documented..

Q-106: B. Maintenance task list and C. Sampling procedure

Inspection points are used if a task list operation requires that multiple pieces of test equipment be inspected and characteristic results for each piece of equipment be recorded. Each inspection point relates to one piece of test equipment and is represented by a unique equipment number. During planning, inspection point data is maintained in the maintenance task list at the header and operation level and in the sampling procedure at the characteristic level. For example, the "inspection points based on equipment" inspection point type must be specified in the task list header and the manual or automatic test equipment valuation control indicator must be selected in the task list operation. In turn, the "inspection points based on inspection lot quantity" identifier must be specified in the sampling procedure that is defined for the inspection characteristic in the maintenance task list.

Q-107:   C. Equipment defined for inspection characteristic

Some test equipment fails shortly after it has been inspected and found to meet the quality specifications defined for the equipment. As a result, a company requires the ability to identify quality inspections that were conducted with the equipment to determine if inspection results obtained with the equipment were valid or if issues with equipment led to erroneous test results. In the latter instance, the company must then determine if the inspections must be repeated. The Test Equipment Tracking Report accommodates this requirement by identifying the inspection characteristics that were evaluated with a particular piece of test equipment. In addition, the tracking report identifies the work center at which an inspection occurred and the time period during which the test equipment was located at the work center.

Q-108:   A. Inspection type assigned to the maintenance order

A maintenance plan is the central planning object for a calibration inspection. The maintenance plan controls the type and scope of inspection activities to be performed, as well as if the activities will be performed on a performance or time-basis. As a maintenance plan is scheduled, maintenance calls are created and a maintenance order is generated. As the maintenance order is created and released, an inspection lot is created based on the inspection type assigned to the maintenance order type and the inspection lot quantity is determined based on the quantity of test equipment that is referenced in the maintenance order. Next, the task list is selected, the calibration inspection is conducted, the inspection results are recorded and the usage decision is documented. The completion of the inspection triggers an update to the equipment status in the equipment master record on the basis of the test equipment valuation documented by the usage decision that is recorded for the inspection lot. In turn, the appraisal activities of the calibration inspection are confirmed for the maintenance order.

Q-109: A. Maintenance order

A maintenance order is created when the proper function of a piece of test equipment must be confirmed. When the order is released, an inspection lot data record is generated. In the process, the inspection specifications for the test equipment are generated, the quantity of equipment to be inspected is confirmed, and inspection characteristics that must be inspected multiple times are identified. At the conclusion of the calibration inspection, results are recorded and the usage decision for the test equipment is documented in the data record using the functions of the Quality Management component

Q-110:   A. Sampling procedure

Samples are taken from a population to determine the characteristics of the population. The inspection of a piece of test equipment in the sample provides a means to verify whether or not the equipment conforms to particular technical specifications and if the test equipment is accepted or rejected for its intended purpose. During this process, one or more characteristics of the equipment may be inspected multiple times and, in turn, repeat measurements documented. These repeat measurements are triggered by the sampling procedure that's assigned to an inspection characteristic, which determines both how the system calculates a sample size and the basis on which an inspection characteristic is valuated.

Q-111:   C. Equipment master record

The entry of a usage decision for an inspection lot concludes the calibration inspection. On the basis of the usage decision code, particular follow-up functions can be triggered. One such follow-up function is the calculation of a quality score for the inspection lot. Other follow-up actions include the update of the inspection interval in the preventive maintenance plan using the cycle modification factor and the creation of measurement documents in which to record the inspection results for measurement points. Also

performed following the conclusion of a calibration inspection are the update of the status of PRT-relevant equipment in the equipment master record to reflect the valuation of the equipment and to control the release of the equipment for future use and the technical completion of a maintenance order, which denotes the completion of planned activities for the maintenance order.

Q-112:   C. QM Change Order

The entry of a usage decision for an inspection lot concludes the calibration inspection. On the basis of the usage decision code, particular follow-up functions can be triggered. One such follow-up function is the calculation of a quality score for the inspection lot. Other follow-up actions include the update of the inspection interval in the preventive maintenance plan using the cycle modification factor and the creation of measurement documents in which to record the inspection results for measurement points. Also performed following the conclusion of a calibration inspection are the update of the status of PRT-relevant equipment in the equipment master record to reflect the valuation of the equipment and to control the release of the equipment for future use and the technical completion of a maintenance order, which denotes the completion of planned activities for the maintenance order.

Q-113:   B. Notification

The results of a calibration inspection are recorded in the system as either characteristic values or defects. A defect record is created in the instance that a particular property of a piece of test equipment does not adhere to a specification that is defined for the inspection characteristic. When the defect record is initially stored in the system, it is assigned two statuses: outstanding quality notification and outstanding defect record. For a critical defect, the outstanding notification can be automatically activated on the basis of a defect class that is assigned to a defect code. Following the activation of the notification, the Notifications functions support the analysis of the origin of the recorded defect and the processing of a resolution to the defect. The notification is completed when the documented issue is resolved. In turn, an outstanding defect record, that pertains to a non-critical issue, is not activated as a notification, but rather is automatically completed when the usage decision for the inspection lot is documented in the system.

Q-114:   A. Preventive Maintenance, B. Plant Maintenance and D. Quality Planning

The functional integration of a business is mirrored in the integration of the Test Equipment Management functions with those of the Quality Management and Plant Maintenance component, each of which support the conduct of calibration inspections. Such components include the PM Technical Objects, PM Preventive Maintenance and PM Maintenance Processing components, the QM Quality Planning and

QM Test Equipment Management components and the Classification System component.

Q-115: A. Create measurement documents for each inspection point defined for the test equipment

The entry of a usage decision for an inspection lot concludes the calibration inspection. On the basis of the usage decision code, particular follow-up functions can be triggered. One such follow-up function is the calculation of a quality score for the inspection lot. Other follow-up actions include the update of the inspection interval in the preventive maintenance plan using the cycle modification factor and the creation of measurement documents in which to record the inspection results for measurement points. Also performed following the conclusion of a calibration inspection are the update of the status of PRT-relevant equipment in the equipment master record to reflect the valuation of the equipment and to control the release of the equipment for future use and the technical completion of a maintenance order, which denotes the completion of planned activities for the maintenance order.

Q-116: C. A maintenance order is completed from a business standpoint following the final posting of costs to the order

A maintenance plan is the central planning object for a calibration inspection. The maintenance plan controls the type and scope of inspection activities to be performed, as well as if the activities will be performed on a performance or time-basis. As a maintenance plan is scheduled, maintenance calls are created and a maintenance order is generated. As the maintenance order is created and released, an inspection lot is created based on the inspection type assigned to the maintenance order type and the inspection lot quantity is determined based on the quantity of test equipment that is referenced in the maintenance order. Next, the task list is selected, the calibration inspection is conducted, the inspection results are recorded and the usage decision is documented. The completion of the inspection triggers an update to the equipment status in the equipment master record on the basis of the test equipment valuation documented by the usage decision that is recorded for the inspection lot. In turn, the appraisal activities of the calibration inspection are confirmed for the maintenance order. The maintenance order is completed from a business standpoint following the final posting of costs to the order.

Q-117:   B. Usage Decision

The entry of a usage decision for an inspection lot concludes the calibration inspection. On the basis of the usage decision code, particular follow-up functions can be triggered. One such follow-up function is the calculation of a quality score for the inspection lot. Other follow-up actions include the update of the inspection interval in the preventive maintenance plan using the cycle modification factor and the creation of measurement documents in which to record the inspection results for measurement points. Also performed following the conclusion of a calibration

211

inspection are the update of the status of PRT-relevant equipment in the equipment master record to reflect the valuation of the equipment and to control the release of the equipment for future use and the technical completion of a maintenance order, which denotes the completion of planned activities for the maintenance order.

Q-118:   B. Enter the inspection point type in the maintenance task list header

Inspection points are used if a task list operation requires that multiple pieces of test equipment be inspected and characteristic results for each piece of equipment be recorded. Each inspection point relates to one piece of test equipment and is represented by a unique equipment number. During planning, inspection point data is maintained in the maintenance task list at the header and operation level and in the sampling procedure at the characteristic level. For example, the "inspection points based on equipment" inspection point type must be specified in the task list header and the manual or automatic test equipment valuation control indicator must be selected in the task list operation. In turn, the "inspection points based on inspection lot quantity" identifier must be specified in the sampling procedure that is defined for the inspection characteristic in the maintenance task list.

Q-119:   A. Inspection type is assigned to the order type

A maintenance plan is the central planning object for a calibration inspection. The maintenance plan controls the type and scope of inspection activities to be performed, as well as if the activities will be performed on a performance or time-basis. As a maintenance plan is scheduled, maintenance calls are created and a maintenance order is generated. As the maintenance order is created and released, an inspection lot is created based on the inspection type assigned to the maintenance order type and the inspection lot quantity is determined based on the quantity of test equipment that is referenced in the maintenance order. Next, the task list is selected, the calibration inspection is conducted, the inspection results are recorded and the usage decision is documented. The completion of the inspection triggers an update to the equipment status in the equipment master record on the basis of the test equipment valuation documented by the usage decision that is recorded for the inspection lot. In turn, the appraisal activities of the calibration inspection are confirmed for the maintenance order.

Q-120:   A. Results Recording Worklist

After the inspection of a piece of test equipment, the inspection results for the individual characteristics that are defined for a task list operation are recorded and compared to predefined specifications. The inspection results for a single inspection lot can be recorded using the Results Recording function. In turn, the inspection results for a number of inspection lots can be recorded using the Results Recording Worklist function.

213

Q-121:   A. Notification type is assigned to the inspection type in Customizing and B. The defects recording control indicator is set in the inspection characteristics

The results of a calibration inspection are recorded in the system as either characteristic values or defects. A defect record is created in the instance that a particular property of a piece of test equipment does not adhere to a specification that is defined for the inspection characteristic. When the defect record is initially stored in the system, it is assigned two statuses: outstanding quality notification and outstanding defect record. For critical defects, the outstanding notification can be automatically activated on the basis of a defect class. Following activation, the Notification functions are used to analyze the origin of a recorded defect and process resolutions to the defects that were originally documented in the defect records. The notification is completed when the documented issue is resolved. In turn, outstanding defect records that pertain to non-critical issues are not activated as a notification. Instead, these records are automatically completed when the usage decision for the inspection lot is entered to the system. The activation of the notification requires the assignment of the maintenance notification type to the calibration inspection type, the selection of the defects recording control indicator for the inspection characteristics and the assignment of a defect class to a defect code.

Q-122:   A. Equipment type is PRT-relevant

The entry of a usage decision for an inspection lot concludes the calibration inspection. On the basis of the usage decision code, particular follow-up functions can be triggered. One such follow-up function is the calculation of a quality score for the inspection lot. Other follow-up actions include the update of the inspection interval in the preventive maintenance plan using the cycle modification factor and the creation of measurement documents in which to record the inspection results for measurement points. Also performed following the conclusion of a calibration inspection are the update of the status of PRT-relevant equipment in the equipment master record to reflect the valuation of the equipment and to control the release of the equipment for future use and the technical completion of a maintenance order, which denotes the completion of planned activities for the maintenance order.

Q-123:   B. Cycle modification factor

A PM maintenance plan is the central planning object for a calibration inspection. The maintenance plan controls the type and scope of inspection activities to be performed and whether the activities are performed on a time or performance-basis. The cycle modification factor is an element of the maintenance plan that is used to alter a plan's time-based or performance-based maintenance cycle to best reflect the actual condition and maintenance requirements of a piece of test equipment. The inspection interval must be revised if the test equipment status, which is documented in the equipment master record, does not reflect the actual

215

condition of the test equipment and if the equipment may require maintenance prior to the next scheduled inspection. In this instance, to preclude the possibility that the equipment may fail prior to the next subsequent inspection, the cycle modification factor in the maintenance plan is changed to reduce the inspection interval as the inspection lot usage decision is documented.

Q-124:   A. Measuring points defined for equipment and B. Linkage of measuring point master records to the master inspection characteristics in the maintenance task list

A usage decision code is entered for an inspection lot at the conclusion of an inspection to document the suitability of test equipment for its intended purpose. The Test Equipment Management system automatically executes particular follow-up actions on the basis of a usage decision code. One such follow-up action is the creation of measurement document for each inspection point that is defined for the test equipment. The results of the calibration inspection are recorded in measurement documents, which are stored in the test equipment history. The requirements of this function include the linkage of the master inspection characteristic in the maintenance task list and the measuring point master records by means of the class characteristics.

Q-125:   B. Release of the maintenance order

A maintenance order is created when the proper function of a piece of test equipment must be confirmed. When the order is released, an inspection lot data record is generated. In the process, the inspection specifications for the test equipment are generated, the quantity of equipment to be inspected is confirmed, and inspection characteristics that must be inspected multiple times are identified.

Q-126:   A. Point that is determined by the user and C. Creation of the inspection lot

An inspector receives information regarding the conduct of a calibration inspection by means of an inspection instruction. This instruction is derived from data in both the inspection plan and the inspection lot. Such data includes the description of the material to be inspected, the inspection date, the inspection lot number and the inspection operations and inspection characteristics. Also included are the inspection method and inspection specifications that are defined for each characteristic. The creation and printout of the instruction is triggered by the calculation of a sample size, the creation of an inspection lot or as determined by the user.

Q-127:   A. Defects recording process and B. Results recording process

The results of a calibration inspection are recorded in the system as either characteristic values or defects. A defect record is created in the instance that a particular property of a piece of test equipment does not adhere to a specification that is defined for the inspection characteristic. When the defect record is initially stored in the system, it is assigned two statuses: outstanding quality notification and outstanding defect record. For critical defects, the outstanding notification can be automatically activated on the basis of a defect class. Following activation, the Notification functions are used to analyze the origin of a recorded defect and process resolutions to the defects that were originally documented in the defect records. The notification is completed when the documented issue is resolved. In turn, outstanding defect records that pertain to non-critical issues are not activated as a notification. Instead, these records are automatically completed when the usage decision for the inspection lot is entered to the system.

Q-128: C. Usage decision process

The entry of a usage decision for an inspection lot concludes the calibration inspection. On the basis of the usage decision code, particular follow-up functions can be triggered. One such follow-up function is the calculation of a quality score for the inspection lot. Other follow-up actions include the update of the inspection interval in the preventive maintenance plan using the cycle modification factor and the creation of measurement documents in which to record the inspection results for measurement points. Also performed following the conclusion of a calibration inspection are the update of the status of PRT-relevant equipment in the equipment master record to reflect the valuation of the equipment and to control the release of the equipment for future use and the technical completion of a maintenance order, which denotes the completion of planned activities for the maintenance order.

Q-129:   C. Usage decision process

The entry of a usage decision for an inspection lot concludes the calibration inspection. On the basis of the usage decision code, particular follow-up functions can be triggered. One such follow-up function is the calculation of a quality score for the inspection lot. Other follow-up actions include the update of the inspection interval in the preventive maintenance plan using the cycle modification factor and the creation of measurement documents in which to record the inspection results for measurement points. Also performed following the conclusion of a calibration inspection are the update of the status of PRT-relevant equipment in the equipment master record to reflect the valuation of the equipment and to control the release of the equipment for future use and the technical completion of a maintenance order, which denotes the completion of planned activities for the maintenance order.

Q-130:   A. Results Recording and Usage Decision functions can trigger follow-up function

The entry of a usage decision or the documentation of inspection results for an inspection lot concludes the calibration inspection. On the basis of the usage decision code, particular follow-up functions can be triggered. One such follow-up function is the calculation of a quality score for the inspection lot. Other follow-up actions include the update of the inspection interval in the preventive maintenance plan using the cycle modification factor and the creation of measurement documents in which to record the inspection results for measurement points. Also performed following the conclusion of a calibration inspection are the update of the status of PRT-relevant equipment in the equipment master record to reflect the valuation of the equipment and to control the release of the equipment for future use and the technical completion of a maintenance order, which denotes the completion of planned activities for the maintenance order.

Q-131:   C. Usage decision process

The entry of a usage decision for an inspection lot concludes the calibration inspection. On the basis of the usage decision code, particular follow-up functions can be triggered. One such follow-up function is the calculation of a quality score for the inspection lot. Other follow-up actions include the update of the inspection interval in the preventive maintenance plan using the cycle modification factor and the creation of measurement documents in which to record the inspection results for measurement points. Also performed following the conclusion of a calibration inspection are the update of the status of PRT-relevant equipment in the equipment master record to reflect the valuation of the equipment and to control the release of the equipment for future use and the technical completion of a maintenance order, which denotes the completion of planned activities for the maintenance order.

Q-132:   B. Results Recording Worklist

After the inspection of a piece of test equipment, the inspection results for the individual characteristics that are defined for a task list operation are recorded and compared to predefined specifications. Inspection results for a single inspection lot can be recorded using the Results Recording function. In turn, the inspection results for a number of inspection lots can be recorded using the Results Recording Worklist function.

Q-133:   A. Maintenance Notification

The results of a calibration inspection are recorded in the system as either characteristic values or defects. A defect record is created in the instance that a particular property of a piece of test equipment does not adhere to a specification that is defined for the inspection characteristic. When the defect record is initially stored in the system, it is assigned two statuses: outstanding quality notification and outstanding defect record. For a critical defect, the outstanding notification can be automatically activated on the basis of a defect class that is assigned to a defect code. Following the activation of the notification, the Notifications functions support the analysis of the origin of the recorded defect and the processing of a resolution to the defect. The notification is completed when the documented issue is resolved. In turn, an outstanding defect record, that pertains to a non-critical issue, is not activated as a notification, but rather is automatically completed when the usage decision for the inspection lot is documented in the system.

Q-134:   A. Test Equipment Tracking Report

Some test equipment fails shortly after it has been inspected and found to meet the quality specifications defined for the equipment. As a result, a company requires the ability to identify quality inspections that were conducted with the equipment to determine if inspection results obtained with the equipment were valid or if issues with equipment led to erroneous test results. In the latter instance, the company must then determine if the inspections must be repeated. The Test Equipment Tracking Report accommodates this requirement by identifying the inspection characteristics that were evaluated with a particular piece of test equipment. In addition, the tracking report identifies the work center at which an inspection occurred and the time period during which the test equipment was located at the work center.

Q-135:   Results Recording

The results of a calibration inspection are recorded in the system as either characteristic values or defects. A defect record is created in the instance that a particular property of a piece of test equipment does not adhere to a specification that is defined for the inspection characteristic. When the defect record is initially stored in the system, it is assigned two statuses: outstanding

222

quality notification and outstanding defect record. For a critical defect, the outstanding notification can be automatically activated on the basis of a defect class that is assigned to a defect code. A maintenance notification item can also be created using a manual process and the Results Recording function.

Q-136:   B. Create and release a maintenance order using a manual process

A maintenance plan is the central planning object for a calibration inspection. The maintenance plan controls the type and scope of inspection activities to be performed, as well as if the activities will be performed on a performance or time-basis. As a maintenance plan is scheduled, maintenance calls are created and a maintenance order is generated. As the maintenance order is created and released, an inspection lot is created based on the inspection type assigned to the maintenance order type. Next, the inspection lot quantity is determined based on the quantity of test equipment that is referenced in the maintenance order. Additional inspection lots can be created using a manual process to create and release additional maintenance orders.

Q-137:   B. Create and release a repair order using an automatic process triggered by the maintenance notification item

The results of a calibration inspection are recorded in the system as either characteristic values or defects. A defect record is created in the instance that a particular property of a piece of test equipment does not adhere to a specification that is defined for the inspection characteristic. When the defect record is initially stored in the system, it is assigned two statuses: outstanding quality notification and outstanding defect record. For a critical defect, the outstanding notification can be automatically activated on the basis of a defect class that is assigned to a defect code. Following the activation of the notification, the Notifications functions support the analysis of the origin of the recorded defect and the processing of a resolution to the defect. The notification is completed when the documented issue is resolved. An automatic process associated with the maintenance notification item can be used to create and release a repair order.

Q-138:   B. Test Equipment Management component

The functional integration of a business is mirrored in the integration of the Test Equipment Management functions with those of the Quality Management and Plant Maintenance components, each of which support the conduct of calibration inspections. Such components include the PM Technical Objects, PM Preventive Maintenance and PM Maintenance Processing components, the QM Quality Planning and QM Test Equipment Management components and the Classification System component.

Q-139:   B. Results Recording Worklist function

After the inspection of a piece of test equipment, the inspection results for the individual characteristics that are defined for a task list operation are recorded and compared to predefined specifications. Inspection results for a single inspection lot can be recorded using the Results Recording function. In turn, inspection results for a number of inspection lots can be recorded using the Results Recording Worklist function.

Q-140:   A. Trigger the creation of a maintenance notification on the basis of the defect code and defect class used to document the defect identified during the inspection

The results of a calibration inspection are recorded in the system as either characteristic values or defects. A defect record is created in the instance that a particular property of a piece of test equipment does not adhere to a specification that is defined for the inspection characteristic. When the defect record is initially stored in the system, it is assigned two statuses: outstanding quality notification and outstanding defect record. For a critical defect, the outstanding notification can be automatically activated on the basis of a defect class that is assigned to a defect code. Following the activation of the notification, the Notifications functions support the analysis of the origin of the recorded defect and the processing of a resolution to the defect. The notification is completed when the documented issue is resolved. In turn, an outstanding defect record, that pertains to a non-critical issue, is not activated as a notification, but rather is automatically completed when the usage decision for the inspection lot is documented in the system. The creation of a maintenance notification item during the results recording process of a calibration inspection requires that the maintenance notification type be assigned to the inspection type using the Customizing application. In addition, the defects recording control indicator must be set for the inspection characteristic.

Q-141:   A. Revise equipment inspection interval

The entry of a usage decision for an inspection lot concludes the calibration inspection. On the basis of the usage decision code, particular follow-up functions can be triggered. One such follow-up function is the calculation of a quality score for the inspection lot. Other follow-up actions include the update of the inspection interval in the preventive maintenance plan using the cycle modification factor and the creation of measurement documents in which to record the inspection results for measurement points. Also performed following the conclusion of a calibration inspection are the update of the status of PRT-relevant equipment in the equipment master record to reflect the valuation of the equipment and to control the release of the equipment for future use and the technical completion of a maintenance order, which denotes the completion of planned activities for the maintenance order.

Q-142:   B. Results Recording

After the inspection of a piece of test equipment, the inspection results for the individual characteristics that are defined for a task list operation are recorded and compared to predefined specifications. Inspection results for a single inspection lot can be recorded using the Results Recording function. In turn, inspection results for a number of inspection lots can be recorded using the Results Recording Worklist function.

Q-143:   B. Definition of inspection interval in maintenance plan

A PM maintenance plan is the central planning object for a calibration inspection. The maintenance plan controls the type and scope of inspection activities to be performed and whether the activities are performed on a time or performance-basis. The cycle modification factor is an element of the maintenance plan that is used to alter a plan's time-based or performance-based maintenance cycle to best reflect the actual condition and maintenance requirements of a piece of test equipment. The inspection interval must be revised if the test equipment status, which is documented in the equipment master record, does not reflect the actual condition of the test equipment and if the equipment may require maintenance prior to the next scheduled inspection.   In this instance, to preclude the possibility that the equipment may fail prior to the next subsequent inspection, the cycle modification factor in the maintenance plan is changed to reduce the inspection interval as the inspection lot usage decision is documented.

Q-144:   C. Document the results of calibration inspection

A usage decision code is entered for an inspection lot at the conclusion of an inspection to document the suitability of test equipment for its intended purpose. The Test Equipment Management system automatically executes particular follow-up actions on the basis of a usage decision code. One such follow-up action is the creation of measurement documents for each inspection point that is defined for the test equipment. In this instance, the results of the calibration inspection are recorded in measurement documents and these documents are stored in the test equipment history. The requirements of this functionality include the linkage of the master inspection characteristic in the maintenance task list and the measuring point master records by means of the class characteristics.

Q-145: A. Test Equipment Tracking Report

Some test equipment fails shortly after it has been inspected and found to meet the quality specifications defined for the equipment. As a result, a company requires the ability to identify quality inspections that were conducted with the equipment to determine if inspection results obtained with the equipment were valid or if issues with equipment led to erroneous test results. In the latter instance, the company must then determine if the inspections must be repeated. The Test Equipment Tracking Report accommodates this requirement by identifying the inspection characteristics that were evaluated with a particular piece of test equipment. In addition, the tracking report identifies the work center at which an inspection occurred and the time period during which the test equipment was located at the work center.

Q-146:   A. Test Equipment Management is integrated with the PM components: Technical Objects, Preventive Maintenance and Plant Maintenance and B. The linkage between QM mast data and the Classification System master date enables the synchronization of data between the system

The functional integration of a business is mirrored in the integration of the Test Equipment Management functions with those of the Quality Management and Plant Maintenance component, each of which support the conduct of calibration inspections. Such components include the PM Technical Objects, PM Preventive Maintenance and PM Maintenance Processing components, the QM Quality Planning and QM Test Equipment Management components and the Classification System component.

Q-147:   A. Create Maintenance Order and C. Create Maintenance Task List

The automatic or manual scheduling of a maintenance plan leads to the creation of a maintenance order for the conduct of a calibration inspection. The release of the maintenance order leads to the creation of the inspection lot and the selection of the maintenance task list to be used for the calibration inspection. Each of these functions occurs during the inspection lot creation phase of a calibration inspection.

Q-148:   A. Shorten the inspection interval by changing the cycle modification factor

A PM maintenance plan is the central planning object for a calibration inspection. The maintenance plan controls the type and scope of inspection activities to be performed and whether the activities are performed on a time or performance-basis. The cycle modification factor is an element of the maintenance plan that is used to alter a plan's time-based or performance-based maintenance cycle to best reflect the actual condition and maintenance requirements of a piece of test equipment. The inspection interval must be revised if the test equipment status, which is documented in the equipment master record, does not reflect the actual condition of the test equipment and if the equipment may require maintenance prior to the next scheduled inspection.   In this instance, to preclude the possibility that the equipment may fail prior to the next subsequent inspection, the cycle modification factor in the maintenance plan is changed to reduce the inspection interval as the inspection lot usage decision is documented.

Q-149:   A. Generate a test equipment tracking report that lists the use of a piece of test equipment at individual work centers as noted in the equipment usage list

Some test equipment fails shortly after it has been inspected and found to meet the quality specifications defined for the equipment. As a result, a company requires the ability to identify quality inspections that were conducted with the equipment to determine if inspection results obtained with the equipment were valid or if issues with equipment led to erroneous test results. In the latter instance, the company must then determine if the inspections must be repeated. The Test Equipment Tracking Report accommodates this requirement by identifying the inspection characteristics that were evaluated with a particular piece of test equipment. In addition, the tracking report identifies the work center at which an inspection occurred and the time period during which the test equipment was located at the work center.

Q-150:   A. Maintenance task list

A maintenance plan is the central planning object for a calibration inspection. The maintenance plan controls the type and scope of inspection activities to be performed, as well as if the activities will be performed on a performance or time-basis. As a maintenance plan is scheduled, maintenance calls are created and a maintenance order is generated. As the maintenance order is created and released, an inspection lot is created and the inspection lot quantity is determined based on the quantity of test equipment that is referenced in the maintenance order. In addition, the task list is selected based on the maintenance task list key stored in the maintenance order, the calibration inspection is conducted, the inspection results are recorded and the usage decision is documented. The completion of the inspection triggers an update to the equipment status in the equipment master record on the basis of the test equipment valuation documented by the usage decision that is recorded for the inspection lot. In turn, the appraisal activities of the calibration inspection are confirmed for the maintenance order.

Q-151:   A. Inspection point

Inspection points are used if a task list operation requires that multiple pieces of test equipment be inspected and characteristic results for each piece of equipment be recorded. Each inspection point relates to one piece of test equipment and is represented by a unique equipment number. During planning, inspection point data is maintained in the maintenance task list at the header and operation level and in the sampling procedure at the characteristic level. For example, the "inspection points based on equipment" inspection point type must be specified in the task list header and the manual or automatic test equipment valuation control indicator must be selected in the task list operation. In turn, the "inspection points based on inspection lot quantity" identifier must be specified in the sampling procedure that is defined for the inspection characteristic in the maintenance task list. In addition, the inspection point key is assigned to the sampling procedure, which identifies the equipment that's subject to a calibration inspection.

Q-152:   A. Linkage of measuring point master records to the master inspection characteristics in the maintenance task list and C. Measuring points defined for equipment

A usage decision code is entered for an inspection lot at the conclusion of an inspection to document the suitability of test equipment for its intended purpose. The Test Equipment Management system automatically executes particular follow-up actions on the basis of a usage decision code. One such follow-up action is the creation of measurement document for each inspection point that is defined for the test equipment. The results of the calibration inspection are recorded in measurement documents, which are stored in the test equipment history. The requirements of this function include the linkage of the master inspection characteristic in the maintenance task list and the measuring point master records by means of the class characteristics.

Q-153:   A. Sampling procedure

Samples are taken from a population to determine the characteristics of the population. The inspection of a piece of test equipment in the sample provides a means to verify whether or not the equipment conforms to particular technical specifications and if the test equipment is accepted or rejected for its intended purpose. During this process, one or more characteristics of the equipment may be inspected multiple times and, in turn, repeat measurements documented. These repeat measurements are triggered by the sampling procedure, which determines both how the system calculates a sample size and the basis on which an inspection characteristic is valuated.

Q-154:   A. Inspection type

A maintenance plan is the central planning object for a calibration inspection. The maintenance plan controls the type and scope of inspection activities to be performed, as well as if the activities will be performed on a performance or time-basis. As a maintenance plan is scheduled, maintenance calls are created and a maintenance order is generated. As the maintenance order is created and released, an inspection lot is created based on the inspection type assigned to the maintenance order type and the inspection lot quantity is determined based on the quantity of test equipment that is referenced in the maintenance order. Next, the task list is selected, the calibration inspection is conducted, the inspection results are recorded and the usage decision is documented. The completion of the inspection triggers an update to the equipment status in the equipment master record on the basis of the test equipment valuation documented by the usage decision that is recorded for the inspection lot. In turn, the appraisal activities of the calibration inspection are confirmed for the maintenance order.

Q-155: A Defects recording control indicator in the inspection characteristic

The results of a calibration inspection are recorded in the system as either characteristic values or defects. A defect record is created in the instance that a particular property of a piece of test equipment does not adhere to a specification that is defined for the inspection characteristic. When the defect record is initially stored in the system, it is assigned two statuses: outstanding quality notification and outstanding defect record. For a critical defect, the outstanding notification can be automatically activated on the basis of a defect class that is assigned to a defect code. This activation requires the assignment of the maintenance notification type to the calibration inspection type, the selection of the defects recording control indicator for the inspection characteristics and the assignment of a defect class to a defect code. Following the activation of the notification, the Notifications functions support the analysis of the origin of the recorded defect and the processing of a resolution to the defect. The notification is completed when the documented issue is resolved. In turn, an outstanding defect record, that pertains to a non-critical issue, is not activated as a notification, but rather is automatically completed when the usage decision for the inspection lot is documented in the system.

Q-156:   A. Class characteristic

Samples are taken from a population to determine the characteristics of the population. The inspection of a piece of test equipment in the sample provides a means to verify whether or not the equipment conforms to particular technical specifications and if the test equipment is accepted or rejected for its intended purpose. During this process, one or more characteristics of the equipment may be inspected multiple times and, in turn, repeat measurements documented. These repeat measurements are triggered by the sampling procedure, which determines both how the system calculates a sample size and the basis on which an inspection characteristic is valuated.

Q-157:   A. Equipment or functional location inspection point type

Inspection points are used if a task list operation requires that multiple pieces of test equipment be inspected and characteristic results for each piece of equipment be recorded. Each inspection point relates to one piece of test equipment and is represented by a unique equipment number. During planning, inspection point data is maintained in the maintenance task list at the header and operation level and in the sampling procedure at the characteristic level. For example, the "inspection points based on equipment" inspection point type must be specified in the task list header and the manual or automatic test equipment valuation control indicator must be selected in the task list operation. In turn, the "inspection points based on inspection lot quantity" identifier must be specified in the sampling procedure that is defined for the inspection characteristic in the maintenance task list.

Q-158:   A. Assignment of plant maintenance inspection type to the maintenance order type

A maintenance plan is the central planning object for a calibration inspection. The maintenance plan controls the type and scope of inspection activities to be performed, as well as if the activities will be performed on a performance or time-basis. As a maintenance plan is scheduled, maintenance calls are created and a maintenance order is generated. As the maintenance order is created and released, an inspection lot is created based on the inspection type assigned to the maintenance order type and the inspection lot quantity is determined based on the quantity of test equipment that is referenced in the maintenance order. Next, the task list is selected, the calibration inspection is conducted, the inspection results are recorded and the usage decision is documented. The completion of the inspection triggers an update to the equipment status in the equipment master record on the basis of the test equipment valuation documented by the usage decision that is recorded for the inspection lot. In turn, the appraisal activities of the calibration inspection are confirmed for the maintenance order.

Q-159: A. Definition of valuation mode for sampling procedure and B. Definition of sampling procedure in inspection characteristic

An inspection is conducted to determine if a material fulfills required quality criteria. To conduct the inspection, physical samples of the material or batch are selected and evaluated according to an inspection plan. Instructions for drawing the sample, such as the size of each physical sample and the number of samples to be taken are documented in a sample-drawing procedure, which is assigned to the inspection plan. The sampling type, which is defined in the sampling procedure, specifies how a sample is to be calculated. For example, 100 percent inspection, fixed sample or a sampling scheme. The sampling procedure also determines the criteria for lot acceptance by means of the valuation mode. Examples of valuation mode include attributive inspection per nonconforming units, variable inspection per s-method and no valuation parameters. The valuation of a characteristic requires the definition of a valuation mode for a sampling procedure and the definition of a sampling procedure in the inspection characteristic.

Q-160:   A. Assignment of maintenance notification type to maintenance inspection type in Customizing and C. Defects recording control indicator in inspection characteristic

The results of a calibration inspection are recorded in the system as either characteristic values or defects. A defect record is created in the instance that a particular property of a piece of test equipment does not adhere to a specification that is defined for the inspection characteristic. When the defect record is initially stored in the system, it is assigned two statuses: outstanding quality notification and outstanding defect record. For a critical defect, the outstanding notification can be automatically activated on the basis of a defect class that is assigned to a defect code. This activation requires the assignment of the maintenance notification type to the calibration inspection type, the selection of the defects recording control indicator for the inspection characteristics and the assignment of a defect class to a defect code. Following the activation of the notification, the Notifications functions support the analysis of the origin of the recorded defect and the processing of a resolution to the defect. The notification is completed when the documented issue is resolved. In turn, an outstanding defect record, that pertains to a non-critical issue, is not activated as a notification, but rather is automatically completed when the usage decision for the inspection lot is documented in the system.

Q-161:   B. Assign test equipment to maintenance task list characteristic and C. Define work center in maintenance task list operation

Some test equipment fails shortly after it has been inspected and found to meet the quality specifications defined for the equipment. As a result, a company requires the ability to identify quality inspections that were conducted with the equipment to determine if inspection results obtained with the equipment were valid or if issues with equipment led to erroneous test results. In the latter instance, the company must then determine if the inspections must be repeated. The Test Equipment Tracking Report accommodates this requirement by identifying the inspection characteristics that were evaluated with a particular piece of test equipment. In addition, the tracking report identifies the work center at which an inspection occurred and the time period during which the test equipment was located at the work center. The creation of the Test Equipment Tracking Report requires the creation of an equipment master record for the test equipment, a reference to the equipment as a production resource tool in the task list operation, the assignment of the test equipment to a characteristic in the task list and the identification of a work center in the task list operation.

239

Q-162: B. Sampling procedure is assigned to the maintenance task list characteristic and C. Link inspection characteristic in task list to measuring point master records by class characteristic

Samples are taken from a population to determine the characteristics of the population. The inspection of a piece of test equipment in the sample provides a means to verify whether or not the equipment conforms to particular technical specifications and if the test equipment is accepted or rejected for its intended purpose. During this process, one or more characteristics of the equipment may be inspected multiple times and, in turn, repeat measurements documented. These repeat measurements are triggered by the sampling procedure that's assigned to an inspection characteristic, which determines both how the system calculates a sample size and the basis on which an inspection characteristic is valuated.

Q-163: B. Assign maintenance notification type to calibration inspection type and C. Set the defects recording control indicator in the inspection characteristic

The results of a calibration inspection are recorded in the system as either characteristic values or defects. A defect record is created in the instance that a particular property of a piece of test equipment does not adhere to a specification that is defined for the inspection characteristic. When the defect record is initially stored in the system, it is assigned two statuses: outstanding quality notification and outstanding defect record. For a critical defect, the outstanding notification can be automatically activated on the basis of a defect class that is assigned to a defect code. This activation requires the assignment of the maintenance notification type to the calibration inspection type, the selection of the defects recording control indicator for the inspection characteristics and the assignment of a defect class to a defect code. Following the activation of the notification, the Notifications functions support the analysis of the origin of the recorded defect and the processing of a resolution to the defect. The notification is completed when the documented issue is resolved. In turn, an outstanding defect record, that pertains to a non-critical issue, is not activated as a notification, but rather is automatically completed when the usage decision for the inspection lot is documented in the system.

Q-164:   A. Equipment master record

A maintenance plan is the central planning object for a calibration inspection. The maintenance plan controls the type and scope of inspection activities to be performed, as well as if the activities will be performed on a performance or time-basis. As a maintenance plan is scheduled, maintenance calls are created and a maintenance order is generated. As the maintenance order is created and released, an inspection lot is created and the inspection lot quantity is determined based on the quantity of test equipment that is referenced in the maintenance order. Next, the task list is selected, the calibration inspection is conducted, the inspection results are recorded and the usage decision is documented. The completion of the inspection triggers an update to the equipment status in the equipment master record on the basis of the test equipment valuation reflected in the usage decision that is documented for the inspection lot. In turn, the appraisal activities of the calibration inspection are confirmed for the maintenance order.

Q-165:   A. Usage Decision

The results of a calibration inspection are recorded in the system as either characteristic values or defects. A defect record is created in the instance that a particular property of a piece of test equipment does not adhere to a specification that is defined for the inspection characteristic. When the defect record is initially stored in the system, it is assigned two statuses: outstanding quality notification and outstanding defect record. For a critical defect, the outstanding notification can be automatically activated on the basis of a defect class that is assigned to a defect code. Following the activation of the notification, the Notifications functions support the analysis of the origin of the recorded defect and the processing of a resolution to the defect. The notification is completed when the documented issue is resolved. In turn, an outstanding defect record, that pertains to a non-critical issue, is not activated as a notification, but rather is automatically completed when the usage decision for the inspection lot is documented in the system.

Q-166:   A. Usage Decision

A maintenance plan is the central planning object for a calibration inspection. The maintenance plan controls the type and scope of inspection activities to be performed, as well as if the activities will be performed on a performance or time-basis. As a maintenance plan is scheduled, maintenance calls are created and a maintenance order is generated. As the maintenance order is created and released, an inspection lot is created based on the inspection type assigned to the maintenance order type and the inspection lot quantity is determined based on the quantity of test equipment that is referenced in the maintenance order. Next, the task list is selected, the calibration inspection is conducted, the inspection results are recorded and the usage decision is documented. The completion of the inspection triggers an update to the equipment status in the equipment master record on the basis of the test equipment valuation documented by the usage decision that is recorded for the inspection lot. In turn, the appraisal activities of the calibration inspection are confirmed for the maintenance order.

Q-167:   A. Sampling procedure

Samples are taken from a population to determine the characteristics of the population. The inspection of a piece of test equipment in the sample provides a means to verify whether or not the equipment conforms to particular technical specifications and if the test equipment is accepted or rejected for its intended purpose. During this process, one or more characteristics of the equipment may be inspected multiple times and, in turn, repeat measurements

243

documented. These repeat measurements are triggered by the sampling procedure that's assigned to an inspection characteristic, which determines both how the system calculates a sample size and the basis on which an inspection characteristic is valuated.

Q-168:   A. Assignment of calibration inspection type to maintenance order type

A maintenance plan is the central planning object for a calibration inspection. The maintenance plan controls the type and scope of inspection activities to be performed, as well as if the activities will be performed on a performance or time-basis. As a maintenance plan is scheduled, maintenance calls are created and a maintenance order is generated. To ensure an inspection lot is created as the maintenance order is created and released, the calibration inspection type is assigned to a maintenance order type. After the inspection lot is created, the inspection lot quantity is determined based on the quantity of test equipment that is referenced in the maintenance order. Next, the task list is selected, the calibration inspection is conducted, the inspection results are recorded and the usage decision is documented. The completion of the inspection triggers an update to the equipment status in the equipment master record on the basis of the test equipment valuation documented by the usage decision that is recorded for the inspection lot. In turn, the appraisal activities of the calibration inspection are confirmed for the maintenance order.

Q-169:   A. Assign the maintenance notification type to the calibration inspection type in the IMG and B. Select the defects recording control indicator for the inspection characteristic

The results of a calibration inspection are recorded in the system as either characteristic values or defects. A defect record is created in the instance that a particular property of a piece of test equipment does not adhere to a specification that is defined for the inspection characteristic. When the defect record is initially stored in the system, it is assigned two statuses: outstanding quality notification and outstanding defect record. For critical defects, the outstanding notification can be automatically activated on the basis of a defect class. Following activation, the Notification functions are used to analyze the origin of a recorded defect and process resolutions to the defects that were originally documented in the defect records. The notification is completed when the documented issue is resolved. In turn, outstanding defect records that pertain to non-critical issues are not activated as a notification. Instead, these records are automatically completed when the usage decision for the inspection lot is entered to the system. The activation of the notification requires the assignment of the maintenance notification type to the calibration inspection type, the selection of the defects recording control indicator for the inspection characteristics and the assignment of a defect class to a defect code.

Q-170:   C. Results Recording Worklist

After the inspection of a piece of test equipment, the inspection results for the individual characteristics that are defined for a task list operation are recorded and compared to predefined specifications. The inspection results for a single inspection lot can be recorded using the Results Recording function. In turn, inspection results for a number of inspection lots can be recorded using the Results Recording Worklist function.

Q-171: C. Notifications

The results of a calibration inspection are recorded in the system as either characteristic values or defects. A defect record is created in the instance that a particular property of a piece of test equipment does not adhere to a specification that is defined for the inspection characteristic. When the defect record is initially stored in the system, it is assigned two statuses: outstanding quality notification and outstanding defect record. For a critical defect, the outstanding notification can be automatically activated on the basis of a defect class that is assigned to a defect code. Following the activation of the notification, the Notifications functions support the analysis of the origin of the recorded defect and the processing of a resolution to the defect. The notification is completed when the documented issue is resolved.

Q-172: B. Plant Maintenance

The functional integration of a business is mirrored in the integration of the Test Equipment Management functions with those of the Quality Management and

Plant Maintenance component, each of which support the conduct of calibration inspections. Such components include the PM Technical Objects, PM Preventive Maintenance and PM Maintenance Processing components, the QM Quality Planning and QM Test Equipment Management components and the Classification System component.

Q-173:   A. Assignment of maintenance notification type to the calibration inspection type in the IMG and B. Entry of the defects recording control indicator in the inspection characteristic

The results of a calibration inspection are recorded in the system as either characteristic values or defects. A defect record is created in the instance that a particular property of a piece of test equipment does not adhere to a specification that is defined for the inspection characteristic. When the defect record is initially stored in the system, it is assigned two statuses: outstanding quality notification and outstanding defect record. For critical defects, the outstanding notification can be automatically activated on the basis of a defect class. Following activation, the Notification functions are used to analyze the origin of a recorded defect and process resolutions to the defects that were originally documented in the defect records. The notification is completed when the documented issue is resolved. In turn, outstanding defect records that pertain to non-critical issues are not activated as a notification. Instead, these records are automatically completed when the usage decision for the inspection lot is entered to the system. The activation of the notification requires the assignment of the maintenance notification type to the calibration inspection type, the selection of the defects recording control indicator for the inspection characteristics and the assignment of a defect class to a defect code.

Q-174: A. Linkage of master inspection characteristics to the measuring point master records by class characteristics

A usage decision code is entered for an inspection lot at the conclusion of an inspection to document the suitability of test equipment for its intended purpose. The Test Equipment Management system automatically executes particular follow-up actions on the basis of a usage decision code. One such follow-up action is the creation of measurement document for each inspection point that is defined for the test equipment. The results of the calibration inspection are recorded in measurement documents, which are stored in the test equipment history. This process requires the creation of equipment master records, the creation of measuring points which reference a general characteristic, the creation of master inspection characteristics with reference to general characteristics, the definition of a maintenance strategy, the creation of a maintenance task list and the creation of a preventive maintenance plan. In addition, the process requires the assignment of the inspection type to the order type, the assignment of the maintenance task list to the order, the selection of the operations control key for the inspection characteristic, the assignment of inspection points to operations and the specification of inspection points in the material task list.

Q-175:   B. Assignment of calibration inspection type to maintenance order type and C. Assignment of maintenance task list to maintenance order

A maintenance plan is the central planning object for a calibration inspection. The maintenance plan controls the type and scope of inspection activities to be performed, as well as if the activities will be performed on a performance or time-basis. As a maintenance plan is scheduled, maintenance calls are created and a maintenance order is generated. As the maintenance order is created and released, an inspection lot is created and the inspection lot quantity is determined based on the quantity of test equipment that is documented in the maintenance order, the task list is selected and the calibration inspection can be conducted. The calibration is conducted and inspection results are recorded. The completion of the inspection, by the entry of the usage decision, triggers an update to the equipment status in the equipment master record on the basis of the test equipment valuation as reflected in the usage decision documented for the inspection lot. In turn, the activities of the calibration inspection are confirmed for the maintenance order. This process requires the creation of equipment master records, the creation of measuring points which reference a general characteristic, the creation of master inspection characteristics with reference to general characteristics, the definition of a maintenance strategy, the creation of a maintenance task list and the creation of a preventive maintenance plan. In addition, the process requires the assignment of the inspection type to the order type, the assignment of the maintenance task list to the order, the selection of the operations control key for the inspection characteristic, the assignment of inspection points to operations and the specification of inspection points in the material task list.

Q-176: A. Define equipment inspection point type in maintenance task list header, B. Define automatic inspection point valuation mode and D. Select the inspection points based on inspection lot quantity control indicator for the sampling procedure

Inspection points are used if a task list operation requires that multiple pieces of test equipment be inspected and characteristic results for each piece of equipment be recorded. Each inspection point relates to one piece of test equipment and is represented by a unique equipment number. During planning, inspection point data is maintained in the maintenance task list at the header and operation level and in the sampling procedure at the characteristic level. For example, the "inspection points based on equipment" inspection point type must be specified in the task list header and the manual or automatic test equipment valuation control indicator must be selected in the task list operation. In turn, the "inspection points based on inspection lot quantity" identifier must be specified in the sampling procedure that is defined for the inspection characteristic in the maintenance task list.

Q-177:   C. Correct the quantity in the maintenance order

A maintenance plan is the central planning object for a calibration inspection. The maintenance plan controls the type and scope of inspection activities to be performed, as well as if the activities will be performed on a performance or time-basis. As a maintenance plan is scheduled, maintenance calls are created and a maintenance order is generated. As the maintenance order is created and released, an inspection lot is created and the inspection lot quantity is determined based on the quantity of test equipment that is referenced in the maintenance order. Next, the task list is selected, the calibration inspection is conducted, the inspection results are recorded and the usage decision is documented. The completion of the inspection triggers an update to the equipment status in the equipment master record on the basis of the test equipment valuation per valuation mode in the maintenance task list and reflected in the usage decision that is documented for the inspection lot. In turn, the appraisal activities of the calibration inspection are confirmed for the maintenance order.

Q-178:   B. Change the valuation mode in the maintenance task list

A maintenance plan is the central planning object for a calibration inspection. The maintenance plan controls the type and scope of inspection activities to be performed, as well as if the activities will be performed on a performance or time-basis. As a maintenance plan is scheduled, maintenance calls are created and a maintenance order is generated. As the maintenance order is created and released, an inspection lot is created and the inspection lot quantity is determined based on the quantity of test equipment that is documented in the maintenance order, the task list is selected and the calibration inspection can be conducted. The calibration is conducted and inspection results are recorded. The completion of the inspection, by the entry of the usage decision, triggers an update to the equipment status in the equipment master record on the basis of the test equipment valuation as reflected in the usage decision documented for the inspection lot. In turn, the activities of the calibration inspection are confirmed for the maintenance order. This process requires the creation of equipment master records, the creation of measuring points which reference a general characteristic, the creation of master inspection characteristics with reference to general characteristics, the definition of a maintenance strategy, the creation of a maintenance task list and the creation of a preventive maintenance plan. In addition, the process requires the assignment of the inspection type to the order type, the assignment of the maintenance task list to the order, the selection of the operations control key for the inspection characteristic, the assignment of inspection points to operations and the specification of inspection points in the material task list.

Q-179: B. Change the cycle modification factor in the maintenance plan to implement a shorter inspection interval

A PM maintenance plan is the central planning object for a calibration inspection. The maintenance plan controls the type and scope of inspection activities to be performed and whether the activities are performed on a time or performance-basis. The cycle modification factor is an element of the maintenance plan that is used to alter a plan's time-based or performance-based maintenance cycle to best reflect the actual condition and maintenance requirements of a piece of test equipment. The inspection interval must be revised if the test equipment status, which is documented in the equipment master record, does not reflect the actual condition of the test equipment and if the equipment may require maintenance prior to the next scheduled inspection. In this instance, to preclude the possibility that the equipment may fail prior to the next subsequent inspection, the cycle modification factor in the maintenance plan is changed to reduce the inspection interval as the inspection lot usage decision is documented.

Q-180: C. Maintenance task list assigned to maintenance order and E. Inspection points assigned to operation

A maintenance plan is the central planning object for a calibration inspection. The maintenance plan controls the type and scope of inspection activities to be performed, as well as if the activities will be performed on a performance or time-basis. As a maintenance plan is scheduled, maintenance calls are created and a maintenance order is generated. As the maintenance order is created and released, an inspection lot is created and the inspection lot quantity is determined based on the quantity of test equipment that is documented in the maintenance order, the task list is selected and the calibration inspection can be conducted. The calibration is conducted and inspection results are recorded. The completion of the inspection, by the entry of the usage decision, triggers an update to the equipment status in the equipment master record on the basis of the test equipment valuation as reflected in the usage decision documented for the inspection lot. In turn, the activities of the calibration inspection are confirmed for the maintenance order. This process requires the creation of equipment master records, the creation of measuring points which reference a general characteristic, the creation of master inspection characteristics with reference to general characteristics, the definition of a maintenance strategy, the creation of a maintenance task list and the creation of a preventive maintenance plan. In addition, the process requires the assignment of the inspection type to the order type, the assignment of the maintenance task list to the order, the selection of the operations control key for the inspection characteristic, the assignment of inspection points to operations and the specification of inspection points in the material task list.

Q-181:   B. Create maintenance task list

A maintenance plan is the central planning object for a calibration inspection. The maintenance plan controls the type and scope of inspection activities to be performed, as well as if the activities will be performed on a performance or time-basis. As a maintenance plan is scheduled, maintenance calls are created and a maintenance order is generated. As the maintenance order is created and released, an inspection lot is created and the inspection lot quantity is determined based on the quantity of test equipment that is documented in the maintenance order, the task list is selected and the calibration inspection can be conducted. The calibration is conducted and inspection results are recorded. The completion of the inspection, by the entry of the usage decision, triggers an update to the equipment status in the equipment master record on the basis of the test equipment valuation as reflected in the usage decision documented for the inspection lot. In turn, the activities of the calibration inspection are confirmed for the maintenance order. This process requires the creation of equipment master records, the creation of measuring points which reference a general characteristic, the creation of master inspection characteristics with reference to general characteristics, the definition of a maintenance strategy, the creation of a maintenance task list and the creation of a preventive maintenance plan. In addition, the process requires the assignment of the inspection type to the order type, the assignment of the maintenance task list to the order, the selection of the operations control key for the inspection characteristic, the assignment of inspection points to operations and the specification of inspection points in the material task list.

Q-182:   A. Inspect test equipment, C. Record inspection results and D. Enter usage decision for inspection lot

A maintenance plan is the central planning object for a calibration inspection. The maintenance plan controls the type and scope of inspection activities to be performed, as well as if the activities will be performed on a performance or time-basis. As a maintenance plan is scheduled, maintenance calls are created and a maintenance order is generated. To ensure an inspection lot is created as the maintenance order is created and released, the calibration inspection type is assigned to a maintenance order type. After the inspection lot is created, the inspection lot quantity is determined based on the quantity of test equipment that is referenced in the maintenance order. Next, the task list is selected, the calibration inspection is conducted, the inspection results are recorded and the usage decision is documented. The completion of the inspection triggers an update to the equipment status in the equipment master record on the basis of the test equipment valuation documented by the usage decision that is recorded for the inspection lot. In turn, the appraisal activities of the calibration inspection are confirmed for the maintenance order.

Q-183:   B. Create measuring points and F. Create preventive maintenance plan

A maintenance plan is the central planning object for a calibration inspection. The maintenance plan controls the type and scope of inspection activities to be performed, as well as if the activities will be performed on a performance or time-basis. As a maintenance plan is scheduled, maintenance calls are created and a maintenance order is generated. As the maintenance order is created and released, an inspection lot is created and the inspection lot quantity is determined based on the quantity of test equipment that is documented in the maintenance order, the task list is selected and the calibration inspection can be conducted. The calibration is conducted and inspection results are recorded. The completion of the inspection, by the entry of the usage decision, triggers an update to the equipment status in the equipment master record on the basis of the test equipment valuation as reflected in the usage decision documented for the inspection lot. In turn, the activities of the calibration inspection are confirmed for the maintenance order. This process requires the creation of equipment master records, the creation of measuring points which reference a general characteristic, the creation of master inspection characteristics with reference to general characteristics, the definition of a maintenance strategy, the creation of a maintenance task list and the creation of a preventive maintenance plan.

Q-184:   A. Schedule preventive maintenance and B. Create and release maintenance order

A maintenance plan is the central planning object for a calibration inspection. The maintenance plan controls the type and scope of inspection activities to be performed, as well as if the activities will be performed on a performance or time-basis. As a maintenance plan is scheduled, maintenance calls are created and a maintenance order is generated. As the maintenance order is created and released, an inspection lot is created and the inspection lot quantity is determined based on the quantity of test equipment that is documented in the maintenance order, the task list is selected and the calibration inspection can be conducted. The automatic creation of the inspection lot requires the assignment of the calibration inspection type to the order type and the assignment of the maintenance task list to the order. The calibration is conducted and inspection results are recorded. The completion of the inspection, by the entry of the usage decision, triggers an update to the equipment status in the equipment master record on the basis of the test equipment valuation as reflected in the usage decision documented for the inspection lot. In turn, the activities of the calibration inspection are confirmed for the maintenance order.

Q-185: A. Inspect test equipment and B. Enter confirmation for maintenance order

A maintenance plan is the central planning object for a calibration inspection. The maintenance plan controls the type and scope of inspection activities to be performed, as well as if the activities will be performed on a performance or time-basis. As a maintenance plan is scheduled, maintenance calls are created and a maintenance order is generated. As the maintenance order is created and released, an inspection lot is created and the inspection lot quantity is determined based on the quantity of test equipment that is documented in the maintenance order, the task list is selected and the calibration inspection can be conducted. The automatic creation of the inspection lot requires the assignment of the calibration inspection type to the order type and the assignment of the maintenance task list to the order. The calibration is conducted and inspection results are recorded. The completion of the inspection, by the entry of the usage decision, triggers an update to the equipment status in the equipment master record on the basis of the test equipment valuation as reflected in the usage decision documented for the inspection lot. In turn, the activities of the calibration inspection are confirmed for the maintenance order.

Q-186:   A. Confirmations are made for maintenance orders

A maintenance plan is the central planning object for a calibration inspection. The maintenance plan controls the type and scope of inspection activities to be performed, as well as if the activities will be performed on a performance or time-basis. As a maintenance plan is scheduled, maintenance calls are created and a maintenance order is generated. As the maintenance order is created and released, an inspection lot is created and the inspection lot quantity is determined based on the quantity of test equipment that is documented in the maintenance order, the task list is selected and the calibration inspection can be conducted. The automatic creation of the inspection lot requires the assignment of the calibration inspection type to the order type and the assignment of the maintenance task list to the order. The calibration is conducted and inspection results are recorded. The completion of the inspection, by the entry of the usage decision, triggers an update to the equipment status in the equipment master record on the basis of the test equipment valuation as reflected in the usage decision documented for the inspection lot. In turn, the activities of the calibration inspection are confirmed for the maintenance order.

Q-187:   A. Inspection point

Inspection points are used if a task list operation requires that multiple pieces of test equipment be inspected and characteristic results for each piece of equipment be recorded. Each inspection point relates to one piece of test equipment and is represented by a unique equipment number. During planning, inspection point data is maintained in the maintenance task list at the header and operation level and in the sampling procedure at the characteristic level. For example, the "inspection points based on equipment" inspection point type must be specified in the task list header and the manual or automatic test equipment valuation control indicator must be selected in the task list operation. In turn, the "inspection points based on inspection lot quantity" identifier must be specified in the sampling procedure that is defined for the inspection characteristic in the maintenance task list.

Q-188:   A. Sampling procedure assigned to the characteristic

Samples are taken from a population to determine the characteristics of the population. In this way, sampling provides the means to verify whether or not the test equipment in the inspection lot conforms to particular

260

technical specifications and if the test equipment is accepted or rejected for its intended purpose. During this process, a characteristic may be inspected multiple times and, in turn, repeat measurements documented. These repeat measurements are triggered by the sampling procedure, which determines both how the system calculates a sample size and the basis on which an inspection characteristic is valuated.

Q-189:   A. Assignment of maintenance notification type to calibration inspection type and B. Selection of the defects recording control indicator for the inspection characteristic

The results of a calibration inspection are recorded in the system as either characteristic values or defects. A defect record is created in the instance that a particular property of a piece of test equipment does not adhere to a specification that is defined for the inspection characteristic. When the defect record is initially stored in the system, it is assigned two statuses: outstanding quality notification and outstanding defect record. For critical defects, the outstanding notification can be automatically activated on the basis of a defect class. Following activation, the Notification functions are used to analyze the origin of a recorded defect and process resolutions to the defects that were originally documented in the defect records. The notification is completed when the documented issue is resolved. In turn, outstanding defect records that pertain to non-critical issues are not activated as a notification. Instead, these records are automatically completed when the usage decision for the inspection lot is entered to the system. The activation of the notification requires the assignment of the maintenance notification type to the calibration inspection type, the selection of the defects recording control indicator for the inspection characteristics and the assignment of a defect class to a defect code.

Q-190: A. Creation of maintenance notification triggered by defect class and B. Creation of repair order triggered by notification item

The results of a calibration inspection are recorded in the system as either characteristic values or defects. A defect record is created in the instance that a particular property of a piece of test equipment does not adhere to a specification that is defined for the inspection characteristic. When the defect record is initially stored in the system, it is assigned two statuses: outstanding quality notification and outstanding defect record. For a critical defect, the outstanding notification can be automatically activated on the basis of a defect class that is assigned to a defect code. Following the activation of the notification, the Notifications functions support the analysis of the origin of the recorded defect and the processing of a resolution to the defect. The notification is completed when the documented issue is resolved. In turn, the maintenance notification can lead to the creation of the equipment repair order.

Q-191: A. Cycle modification factor in the preventive maintenance plan

A PM maintenance plan is the central planning object for a calibration inspection. The maintenance plan controls the type and scope of inspection activities to be performed and whether the activities are performed on a time or performance-basis. The cycle modification factor is an element of the maintenance plan that is used to alter a plan's time-based or performance-based maintenance cycle to best reflect the actual condition and maintenance requirements of a piece of test equipment. The inspection interval must be revised if the test equipment status, which is documented in the equipment master record, does not reflect the actual condition of the test equipment and if the equipment may require maintenance prior to the next scheduled inspection. In this instance, to preclude the possibility that the equipment may fail prior to the next subsequent inspection, the cycle modification factor in the maintenance plan is changed to reduce the inspection interval as the inspection lot usage decision is documented.

Q-192:   A. The test equipment is designated a production resource tool at the task list operation level and C. Equipment master records have been defined for the test equipment

Some test equipment fails shortly after it has been inspected and found to meet the quality specifications defined for the equipment. As a result, a company requires the ability to identify quality inspections that were conducted with the equipment to determine if inspection results obtained with the equipment were valid or if issues with equipment led to erroneous test results. In the latter instance, the company must then determine if the inspections must be repeated. The Test Equipment Tracking Report accommodates this requirement by identifying the inspection characteristics that were evaluated with a particular piece of test equipment. In addition, the tracking report identifies the work center at which an inspection occurred and the time period during which the test equipment was located at the work center. The creation of the Test Equipment Tracking Report requires the creation of an equipment master record for the test equipment, a reference to the equipment as a production resource tool in the task list operation, the assignment of the test equipment to a characteristic in the task list and the identification of a work center in the task list operation.

Q-193:   B. PM Preventive Maintenance and D. Classification System

The functional integration of a business is mirrored in the integration of the Test Equipment Management functions with those of the Quality Management and Plant Maintenance component, each of which support the conduct of calibration inspections. Such components include the PM Technical Objects, PM Preventive Maintenance and PM Maintenance Processing components, the QM Quality Planning and QM Test Equipment Management components and the Classification System component.

Q-194:   A. Manual entry of the usage decision code for one single inspection lot, B. Manual entry of the usage decision code for more than one single inspection lot with the work list function, C. Automatic entry of the usage decision code for one single inspection lot and D. Automatic entry of the usage decision code for more than one single inspection lot

A periodic calibration inspection is conducted to determine the condition of a piece of test equipment The inspection ensures that adverse factors that are discovered during an inspection, which affect the valuation of test equipment, are documented and drawn to the attention of management. During the inspection, inspection results are recorded as either characteristic values or defects. The equipment valuation that follows the inspection reflects a company's decision to accept or reject a piece of equipment for its intended purpose on the basis of the inspection results documented during the calibration inspection. Following the entry of the usage decision for the inspection lot, the status of the test equipment, which is maintained in the Material Master Record, is updated. The valuation of characteristics and the test equipment can be performed using a manual or automatic Results Recording function. These functions include the manual entry of the usage decision code for one single inspection lot, the manual entry of the usage decision code for more than one single inspection lot with the work list function, the automatic entry of the usage decision code for one single inspection lot and the automatic entry of the usage decision code for more than one single inspection lot.

Q-195: A. Manual or proposed entry of the test equipment status and C. Manual or automatic creation of measurement documents

The entry of a usage decision for an inspection lot concludes the calibration inspection. On the basis of the usage decision code, particular follow-up functions can be triggered. One such follow-up function is the calculation of a quality score for the inspection lot. Other follow-up actions include the update of the inspection interval in the preventive maintenance plan using the cycle modification factor and the creation of measurement documents in which to record the inspection results for measurement points. Also performed following the conclusion of a calibration inspection are the update of the status of PRT-relevant equipment in the equipment master record to reflect the valuation of the equipment and to control the release of the equipment for future use and the technical completion of a maintenance order, which denotes the completion of planned activities for the maintenance order.

Q-196: A. Cycle modification factor

A PM maintenance plan is the central planning object for a calibration inspection. The maintenance plan controls the type and scope of inspection activities to be performed and whether the activities are performed on a time or performance-basis. The cycle modification factor is an element of the maintenance plan that is used to alter a plan's time-based or performance-based maintenance cycle to best reflect the actual condition and maintenance requirements of a piece of test equipment. The inspection interval must be revised if the test equipment status, which is documented in the equipment master record, does not reflect the actual condition of the test equipment and if the equipment may require maintenance prior to the next scheduled inspection. In this instance, to preclude the possibility that the equipment may fail prior to the next subsequent inspection, the cycle modification factor in the maintenance plan is changed to reduce the inspection interval as the inspection lot usage decision is documented.

Q-197: A. Master record maintained for the individual piece of test equipment and B. Support for the periodic calibration of test equipment

A periodic calibration inspection is conducted to determine the condition of a piece of test equipment The inspection ensures that adverse factors that are discovered during an inspection, which affect the valuation of test equipment, are documented and drawn to the attention of management. During the inspection, inspection results are recorded as either characteristic values or defects. The equipment valuation that follows the inspection reflects a company's decision to accept or reject a piece of equipment for its intended purpose on the basis of the inspection results documented during the calibration inspection. Following the entry of the usage decision for the inspection lot, the status of the test equipment, which is maintained in the Material Master Record, is updated. The valuation of characteristics and the test equipment can be performed using a manual or automatic Results Recording function.

Q-198:   A. Test Equipment Tracking Report

Some test equipment fails shortly after it has been inspected and found to meet the quality specifications defined for the equipment. As a result, a company requires the ability to identify quality inspections that were conducted with the equipment to determine if inspection results obtained with the equipment were valid or if issues with equipment led to erroneous test results. In the latter instance, the company must then determine if the inspections must be repeated. The Test Equipment Tracking Report accommodates this requirement by identifying the inspection characteristics that were evaluated with a particular piece of test equipment. In addition, the tracking report identifies the work center at which an inspection occurred and the time period during which the test equipment was located at the work center.

Q-199:   A. Defects Recording, B. Results Recording and C. Usage Decision

A maintenance plan is the central planning object for a calibration inspection. The maintenance plan controls the type and scope of inspection activities to be performed, as well as if the activities will be performed on a performance or time-basis. As a maintenance plan is scheduled, maintenance calls are created and a maintenance order is generated. As the maintenance order is created and released, an inspection lot is created based on the inspection type assigned to the maintenance order type and the inspection lot quantity is determined based on the quantity of test equipment that is referenced in the maintenance order. Next, the task list is selected, the calibration inspection is conducted, the inspection results are recorded and the usage decision is documented. The completion of the inspection triggers an update to the equipment status in the equipment master record on the basis of the test equipment valuation documented by the usage decision that is recorded for the inspection lot. In turn, the appraisal activities of the calibration inspection are confirmed for the maintenance order. The Results Recording, Defects Recording and Usage Decision functions can be used to post activity times to the PM maintenance order.

Q-200:   Usage Decision

The entry of a usage decision for an inspection lot concludes the calibration inspection. On the basis of the usage decision code, particular follow-up functions can be triggered. One such follow-up function is the calculation of a quality score for the inspection lot. Other follow-up actions include the update of the inspection interval in the preventive maintenance plan using the cycle modification factor and the creation of measurement documents in which to record the inspection results for measurement points. Also performed following the conclusion of a calibration inspection are the update of the status of PRT-relevant equipment in the equipment master record to reflect the valuation of the equipment and to control the release of the equipment for future use and the technical completion of a maintenance order, which denotes the completion of planned activities for the maintenance order.

Q-201:   B. Equipment Master Record

The entry of a usage decision for an inspection lot concludes the calibration inspection. On the basis of the usage decision code, particular follow-up functions can be triggered. One such follow-up function is the calculation of a quality score for the inspection lot. Other follow-up actions include the update of the inspection interval in the preventive maintenance plan using the cycle modification factor and the creation of measurement documents in which to record the inspection results for measurement points. Also performed following the conclusion of a calibration inspection are the update of the status of PRT-relevant equipment in the equipment master record to reflect the valuation of the equipment and to control the release of the equipment for future use and the technical completion of a maintenance order, which denotes the completion of planned activities for the maintenance order.

www.ingramcontent.com/pod-product-compliance
Lightning Source LLC
Chambersburg PA
CBHW070939050326
40689CB00014B/3268